A Guide to Writing Academic Essays in Religious Studies

A Guide to Writing Academic Essays in Religious Studies

Scott G. Brown

continuum

Continuum International Publishing Group

The Tower Building   80 Maiden Lane
11 York Road   Suite 704
London SE1 7NX   New York NY 10038

www.continuumbooks.com

First published 2008

British Library Cataloguing-in-Publication Data
A catalogue record for this book is available from the British Library.

ISBN-10: HB: 0-8264-9887-6
       PB: 0-8264-9888-4
ISBN-13: HB: 978-0-8264-9887-8
       PB: 978-0-8264-9888-5

Library of Congress Cataloging-in-Publication Data
Brown, Scott G.
  A Guide to writing academic essays in religious studies / Scott G. Brown.
     p. cm
  Includes bibliographical references and indexes.
  ISBN 978-0-8264-9887-8 – ISBN 978-0-8264-9888-5 1.
Religious literature–Authorship. I. Title.

  BL41.B76 2008
  200.71'1–dc22   2007031122

Typeset by YHT Ltd, London
Printed and bound in Great Britain by MPG Books Ltd, Bodmin, Cornwall

Contents

Foreword

Many students arrive at the university keen but somewhat unprepared. Faced with this reality, university professors and teaching assistants have worked harder to impart their storehouses of scholarship, since the intellectual tools, such as essay writing, that help students integrate this knowledge are often starkly absent. Quite pragmatically, Scott G. Brown has begun to address this situation in this wonderfully written, accessible book *A Guide to Writing Academic Essays in Religious Studies*. This guide will help both students and professors: the latter would do well to assign it as compulsory reading, whereas the former would do well to read it and reread it, studying it as one should such essentials of the academic trade as William Strunk Jr. and E. B. White's *Elements of Style*, or Howard S. Becker's *Writing for Social Scientists*.

All academics to some degree work in and with language. It is an essential and basic building block that cannot be emphasized enough. By helping students become more comfortable with writing, as a means both of thinking and of expressing thought, works such as Brown's are akin to a saving grace: many budding intellects will likely better succeed because of this book, whereas without it – the alternative is unpleasant to contemplate. Professors and teaching assistants know all too well what scholarship without regard to form looks like, and far too many students discover how such work is graded, much to their dismay!

I remember when I was a young student of comparative religions myself, an esteemed professor, Pierluigi Piovanelli, telling me about Brown's essay on essay writing in Religious Studies. To both I owe a significant academic and intellectual debt. Many of the methodological and theoretical questions that still fascinate me today first emerged while studying Brown's essay, comparing it to works about essay writing in other fields. Indeed, this comparison – between essay writing in Religious Studies and essay writing in other fields – is a good way to begin contemplating Religious Studies' academic specificity. Brown makes important distinctions in this regard, so as to make plain in the minds of his readers that a Religious Studies essay is not an opinion piece, a simple response to materials covered in class, but rather a serious and methodical scholarly engagement with human creations, built upon the researches of prior generations of scholarship.

Religious Studies is a difficult field because religion itself, its subject matter, too often encourages students to think less rather than more. Acknowledging the field's difficulties, Brown, like all good teachers of Religious Studies, invites his readers to overcome this tendency and to strive to move beyond their inhibitions towards broader horizons of the mind and spirit, where honest intellectual discourses about religion are welcomed, even enthusiastically promoted. For having put together such an essential pedagogical instrument as this, one that will benefit generations of future Religious Studies scholars, the international community of students of religion owe Scott Brown their sincere thanks and appreciation.

Mathieu E. Courville,
Canadian Corporation for the Study of Religion
(CCSR) Graduate Student Representative 2004–2007

Preface

This guide explains various aspects of essay writing that undergraduate students are rarely specifically taught. The academic format described here is best suited to research essays involving the use of historical documents (primary sources) and the books and articles scholars have written on these texts (secondary sources) and is not, therefore, the proper format for every religion essay. Although the directives offered in this guide are fairly standard, they will at times conflict with your professor's views and preferences, particularly concerning matters of style and the theoretical assumptions made in Religious Studies. Thus, if you came across this guide on your own, it is best to ask your instructor whether it is suitable for the course you are taking and to follow any modifications that your instructor wishes to make.

I believe that most undergraduate students have neither the time nor the inclination to read a long book on how to write an essay. Indeed, I know from experience that the students who most need to read this guide are the ones who are most likely to be put off by a big book that tries to explain everything. Accordingly, this book focuses on the essentials, paying special attention to the common and the costly mistakes. The first section is directed to students who are taking their first course in Religious Studies. It roughly corresponds to the original version of this guide, which I produced as a teaching assistant in 1997. Like most graders in the introductory survey course, I hated giving intelligent students low grades because they misunderstood what we expected of them and made some fatal mistakes. So after receiving numerous sermons, apologetic papers, and forays into moral issues; papers with no discernible thesis; and papers with no discernible documentation, I decided to spell out the things that Western instructors in public universities expect their students to figure out by the time the first term paper is due. My main concern was to clarify the difference between religious essays and academic essays about religion for the benefit of students who mistakenly thought that a 'religion essay' is supposed to give the student's personal opinion about the truth of some religious issue. This part of the guide covers most of what students need to know in order to write a good essay for a first- or second-year religion course. It is now followed by a section on how to approach ancient texts, which outlines issues of interpretation that are more basic than the formal practice of exegesis.

The remainder of the guide is geared to students who continue on in a Religious Studies programme. Although new students should be able to understand these sections, they introduce matters of writing and scholarship that become more important in the last year or two of an undergraduate degree and first-year graduate school. The section on the hallmarks of bad scholarship surveys the common forms of illogic and the many subtle forms of intellectual dishonesty that scholars who endorse problematic positions use to level the playing field. I believe that people who consciously reflect on these things are much less likely to commit errors in reasoning or to give in to those partly subconscious temptations to misrepresent. The discussion of logical fallacies in this section will be more relevant to undergraduate students than will the preceding discussion of how scholars make bad arguments look good, which was composed with young graduate students in mind.

Various people took an interest in this guide at different stages in its evolution. I want to thank Larry Schmidt and Harold Remus for their constructive critiques; Terry Tak-ling Woo and George Chryssides for helping me widen the scope of examples; William Closson James and Russell T. McCutcheon for their efforts to widen this guide's audience; and Mathieu E. Courville for composing the foreword and directing me to the right publisher. An earlier version was published in *The Council of Societies for the Study of Religion Bulletin* 28 (1999): 69–76.

Note to the Reader

This guide follows British conventions of spelling and punctuation, but switches to American punctuation when illustrating the conventions of documentation prescribed in *The Chicago Manual of Style*. Since students in most Commonwealth countries are encouraged to use 'British' punctuation in their essays (including the documentation), and North American students are encouraged to use 'American' punctuation, I recommend that students who are unsure of the differences between American and British punctuation start with the explanations provided in the sections on documentation and style.

1 The Essentials of Essay Writing, for Students New to Religious Studies

What Is an Academic Essay?

In order to write a good essay it is customary to develop a thesis, which is a particular proposition to be argued. Essays are not general discussions of a topic, like those found in a textbook. Ideally, they are arguments of a particular point that you consider to be correct and worth making. To begin an essay you should do extensive reading on a specific, as yet unresolved (or too facilely resolved) topic, critically assess the positions of the authors you consult, and then integrate their findings and your own insights into a paper that presents your considered opinion on the matter. The first paragraph (or so) briefly outlines the issue your paper addresses then presents a clearly formulated thesis statement describing your position. The body of the essay attempts to demonstrate the validity of your thesis through a logical progression of arguments. The final paragraphs sum up what you have demonstrated and comment on its relevance.

Essays, then, do not just summarize handbook discussions of a topic, nor do they just repeat the standard arguments for an established position. They are attempts to convince others that your way of conceptualizing a matter is correct. The mode of presentation for an essay is therefore analytical: by examining the relevant evidence, you show that your thesis better accounts for the facts than do the competing theses. Alternatively, you may endeavour to prove only that one particular thesis or theory is false. The thesis of your paper need not be original. It may be a position that you encountered in your research, or an adaptation of a position.

That is, you might be taking sides in a debate, arguing that a thesis or theory offered by one scholar or group of scholars best explains the data.

This argumentative approach is the standard format for a research paper. It is the format one comes across most often in articles published in academic journals. The argumentative essay is the best format to showcase your ability to think critically and independently. It is not, however, the only way to write an essay. A variation on this format is what might be called the exploratory essay, which starts with a problem, intensively analyses the evidence, then reaches a conclusion (i.e. what otherwise would be the thesis) at the end. Some people prefer to write a paper this way because it allows them to review all the evidence systematically, thereby conveying to their readers that their own assessment is not controlling and biasing their analysis, leading them to conceal evidence they cannot explain. While the motive is com- mendable, this procedure can sometimes make your paper harder to understand, for it involves a lengthier presentation of the evidence and may leave your reader wondering what all this analysis is leading up to. Having a thesis statement may engender better organization and clearer communica- tion of your thoughts, for the structure of the paper will be determined by whatever would be the most logical pro- gression of the arguments and discussions that substantiate your case.

Another sort of essay discusses the origin and development of some aspect of a religion, for instance the evolution of the Hindu god Shiva, or of the practice of sati, or of the Jewish and Christian conceptions of Satan. Such issues usually do not lend themselves to the formulation of a single thesis statement because many disparate factors may contribute to a sequence of historical changes, and each must be analysed individually. Because the scope of these essays is broad and the subjects of analysis are not always controversial, essays like these do not always provide as good a forum for demonstrating your ability to think for yourself. It might be better to discuss only one stage in the development of some feature of a religion, particularly a stage about which there is some dispute.

One type of essay deserves mention as an example of what you should not produce: a descriptive essay offering standard information about a religion. Do you remember when you were in junior high school and your teacher told you to write a report on some topic, whereupon you went to the library, opened up the encyclopedia, and tried to put the information into your own words? Your intellect has by now surpassed that challenge. A university research essay is not just newly repackaged information. An essay that offers a mere description of 'The Shinto Religion' or 'The Five Ks of Sikhism' or 'The Four Noble Truths of Buddhism' might not receive a passing grade.

In addition to these general kinds of essays, there are special types of essays that rely on the standard argumentative approach. One might choose to do a comparative essay, that is, an essay that compares two religious traditions with respect to a particular subject. One might compare Buddhist and Hindu understandings of rebirth, Buddhist and Christian understandings of the essence of a human, or Israel and Pakistan as two religious states. Essays of this sort still require a thesis or at least a 'point' to be made. Noting similarities and differences between two religions is a useless endeavour unless something meriting argument can be demonstrated through this comparison. Thus the comparison must have a definite focus, and the analysis of similarities and differences should substantiate some larger insight, which would be the thesis of the paper.

Another specific type of essay is the exegetical essay. The word *exegesis* derives from a Greek word meaning 'to lead out'. The term refers to established methods of interpretation designed to draw the author's meaning *out of* a text. The systematic approaches of exegesis are a means of countering the natural tendency to read one's own presuppositions *into* religious texts (which is called eisegesis). An exegetical paper explains the meaning of a particular passage of scripture, or of a group of related passages. Such essays are arguments about what the writer of the passage meant these words to convey. An exegetical essay might, for example, explain a perplexing passage, such as the comment in the Gospel of Mark that Jesus taught the crowds in parables so that they would not understand him (4:10–12); or it might explain what a particular author meant by a particular phrase or concept through an analysis of all the passages in which that phrase or concept occurs. Again, these essays should have a thesis. Unlike commentaries on scripture, exegetical papers do not go sentence by sentence through the passage explaining every thought in order. The structure of an exegetical essay should correspond to the most logical and compelling pre-sentation of evidence and arguments that support a particular interpretation. It is essential to engage other scholars' inter-pretations of the passage and to show that they are less adequate interpretations by pointing out features of the passage that they cannot explain.

The Methodological and Theoretical Presuppositions of Religious Studies

In public universities, the study of religion is an academic rather than a religious exercise. We are not out to defend or refute the spiritual values and beliefs of the religions we investigate, for such things are not usually open to scientific inquiry. Instead, we set metaphysical and supernatural mat-ters aside and concentrate on what can be learned about religious phenomena through the 'secular' avenues of investigation used in the humanities. This is not to suggest that academic scholarship seeks to 'explain away' religious realities or to reduce them entirely to factors that are not religious. Rather, it is to affirm that *all* aspects of human behaviour and experience are influenced by forces that *are* open to scientific investigation (e.g. social, psychological, economic, cultural, and political forces) – regardless of whether other scientifically inscrutable factors are involved. Thus, scholars investigate the religious dimension of human behaviour using the very same methods, theories, and assumptions that academics use to study human nature in the humanities and social sciences. The tools of historiography, anthropology, sociology, literary criticism, and so forth may not tell us everything we want to know about religion. Indeed, a strictly academic approach is not apt to shed light upon the ultimate questions of human existence. But for pragmatic reasons, metaphysical investigations of religious truths are best conducted in places where all persons involved already agree upon a set of theological pre-suppositions, and that kind of consensus rarely occurs outside of academic communities that are based on religious affilia-tion, such as seminaries, Bible colleges, university theology departments, Jewish yeshivot (rabbinic academies), Hindu theological colleges, and meditation groups. In a context that is as religiously pluralistic as a public university, researchers cannot derive axioms from their faith, support their claims through appeal to revelation or dogma, or cite scripture as an authority that is above question. Rather, they are obliged to limit themselves to theoretical assumptions, methods, forms of argument, and kinds of evidence that are open to scrutiny and challenge by anyone. Thus scholars make an effort to step outside of their own religious presuppositions and allow reason and logic to function as generally accepted standards for truth. The institutional endeavour to develop and refine a common, empirically based set of presuppositions is what permits researchers of differing faiths to communicate meaningfully and reach the kind of consensus that furthers the academic enterprise.

It follows that scholars who work in public universities are not trying to comprehend religions in the ways that religions tend to comprehend themselves, in terms of encounters between the supernatural and the human. Rather than considering intangible forces such as enlightenment, divine inspiration, revelation, and divine intervention, scholars focus on tangible factors discernible within the larger social-historical context. At first blush, this restriction of the academic study of religion to what is tangible and measurable might seem to misconstrue the essence of religion. But whatever that essence might be (the question is endlessly debated), religion involves more than spirituality and cannot be fully comprehended without reference to those other, more down-to-earth qualities. When you examine religious ideas and practices within their historical contexts, they become less mystifying, more intelligible. Metaphysical systems lose some of the ethereal quality of disembodied thoughts. And the proponents of these systems cease to appear simply as hallowed beings who had a special revelation of the truth and the moral fortitude to proclaim it. The academic approach enables us to appreciate the ways in which the founders of religious movements were culturally conditioned individuals who, like ourselves, accepted most of the prevailing assumptions of their societies. And it enables us to appreciate how the new and influential aspects of their teachings had social and political relevance to that time and place.

Traditional accounts of the origins of religious customs and beliefs usually envision godly teachers who either brought eternal truth down from heaven (e.g. Krishna, Jesus, Sun Myung Moon), received it as a revelation from above (Moses, Zoroaster, the Jewish prophets, Muhammad, Nanak, Baha'u'llah, Joseph Smith), acquired access to it through some rite or procedure (shamans, magicians), or managed through discipline to transcend their own culture and humanity to a point where they could see ultimate reality as it truly is (the Buddha, Mahavira). Whatever truth there is to these conceptions, we should not let them preclude historical analysis of the formative thinkers and texts, and obscure the relationship between religious truth and the shape of society. This relationship is obscured not only by explanations of religion that appeal to revelation and enlightenment, but also by explanations that attribute religious customs and ideals to a religious leader's personal dispositions and beliefs. Explaining that a particular leader ordained something because he or she believed something is a circular explanation unless that belief is itself accounted for as a reasonable response to particular circumstances. Saying, for instance, that the Buddha had no regard for the caste system because he *believed* that anyone can attain enlightenment is an empty, circular explanation. For it does not explain why, as a person living in a particular set of circumstances in a particular time and place, he might have been disposed to see the matter that way. Noting that his disregard for caste was part of a wider rejection of aspects of Brahmanism (e.g. the authority of the Vedas, expensive animal sacrifices) that undergirded an inequitable social structure in artificial dependency upon the priestly class – *that* is an historical explanation (whether or not it is the best one).

It is useful to consider how religious ideas can *do* things. Whereas entrenched religious ideals tend to preserve the status quo, new or revived ideals often empower social change. When religious thinkers reject the metaphysical basis of one system of thought in favour of another, they are often producing a new world-view or system of meaning that entails a revised social order. The introduction of a new cosmology (i.e. a new view of the 'shape' of the universe and of our places within it) through the promotion of a new doctrine can result in tangible benefits to the adherents, which in turn help explain the popularity of a tradition. For example, being a Buddhist in the fifth century BCE could raise the social status of a person from a lower *varna* (class) and make possible the pursuit of social and religious goals that were being curtailed by Brahmanism. Students studying the origins of theistic religions (e.g. the teachings of Zoroaster, Moses, Jesus, Muhammad, or the Sikh gurus) are especially likely to overlook the social, political, and economic factors that made these new messages attractive. The 'pipeline' model of revelation is so deeply entrenched in these traditions (and much of the scholarship on them) that people seldom think to ask *why* these founders might themselves have embraced the messages they proclaimed, and why so many people responded to them.

It is important to be very clear about the proper methods and subject matter of academic investigation in a public university because the writing of *religious* or *theological* essays is a common and costly mistake. Each year teachers and graders in introductory religion courses receive essays exploring questions such as: What is the truest form of Sikhism? Is Jesus the Son of God? Should Muslim women wear the veil? And so on. These may all be stimulating questions, and the essays produced may be judged to be very good *in a religious or theological context*; but they frequently result in a failing grade because they do not offer the marker a chance to evaluate the breadth of the student's research into the academic literature and ability to analyse an issue according to the methods of that scholarship. It *is* possible to study the ideas of theologians and other religious thinkers without *doing* theology yourself, provided you take a disinterested, third-person perspective and consider these ideas as social phenomena, intelligible within that particular time and place. *But if you have difficulty viewing your own religion the way that scholars investigate 'other people's' beliefs, then write your essay on another religion* (if that is an option). Researching a religion of which you are not a participant is the safest option, particularly considering that students new to university Religious Studies find it very difficult to recognize when they are assuming things that scholars would not accept. What scholars have concluded about a matter and what people are taught about that matter through their religious education are often very different things.

What You Can Assume about Your Grader's Background Knowledge

Students are often unsure about what information or assumptions they can take for granted in their essay and what they need to define, explain, or argue. For survey courses on the world's religions, it is generally best to presume only that your grader knows and accepts the information and hypotheses about a particular religion that are offered in the course readings and lectures. That means that if you select a topic not covered in the course itself, you will need to do more explaining than usual. In North America, the graders in World Religions courses are often graduate students who specialize in one particular period of one religion. The professors in these survey courses usually have more general knowledge about religions, but are also not experts in all religions. You can get some sense of how much your grader knows about your topic by discussing your paper with him or her while you are still researching it. If you know that you will be evaluated by someone who has studied your topic (as is more typically the case in higher-level courses), you can explain less. Bear in mind that it must be evident that *you* know the meanings, relevant dates, and so forth of the terms you are using. If that is not apparent to your grader through the cogency of your discussion, he or she will likely write comments such as 'define' or 'explain' (the same applies for tests).

How Is an Essay Evaluated?

Your grader will attempt to assess the extent of your research and learning on the topic; the amount of independent, critical reflection that preceded your solution; and the reasonableness and intellectual integrity of your arguments. Your ability to express your thoughts clearly and effectively in an organized and compelling manner will also be assessed, as will the completeness and correctness of the paper's documentation. The grading covers both form and content.

Content

The content is the most important thing. It should demonstrate extensive learning and intelligent analysis. Academic inquiry aims to advance the state of knowledge within a particular field. Thus the quality of this analysis is evaluated, not the character of the person who produced it. *Academic* essay writing is not a forum for defending personal or religious convictions or for disclosing one's private thoughts. The writer of a research essay engages in the impersonal exercise of analysing a phenomenon in order to gain some rational understanding of its occurrence. The persuasiveness of the argument should therefore be logical rather than rhetorical, aimed at the intellect and not the heart. Appeals to the emotions or to religious values not only are out of place in academic writing but actually weaken one's position, for by relying on these things one is tacitly acknowledging that the evidence does not provide sufficiently strong support.

Though logic and reason constitute the primary instruments of investigation, the analysis is more impressive if it is conducted within the framework of an established theory. You might, for example, do a Marxist analysis of the Hindu class system, a Durkheimian analysis of the Protestant work ethic, a Weberian analysis of a religion's institutional structure, or a Jungian (or some sort of literary-critical) analysis of a passage of scripture. The attention you need to give to method and theory will increase as you advance through a Religious Studies programme.

Whether or not you adopt a particular methodology, you will not have adequately examined an issue until you have fully situated it in its historical context. The tell-tale signs of weak historical perspective include the substitution of vague phrases, inductive generalizations (sweeping conclusions based on a few examples), and casual inferences for specific social-historical description. It does not suffice to state that something happened 'in ancient times', or to explain that particular texts were composed by 'the religious elites'. Be as specific as possible. Note when things happened, who were involved, and which sect or branch of the religion is at issue. All religions change over time: like branches on a tree, new forms develop with new sets of rituals and beliefs. Thus one should not assume that, for instance, all East Asian Buddhists accepted the same basic texts and beliefs associated with the Theravada school in India. Even the supposedly fundamental beliefs of a religion are not interpreted the same way within every form of the religion. So focus on the *particular* beliefs and practices of the particular branch of the religion you are investigating.

One familiar assumption reflecting inadequate historical consciousness deserves special mention. Some students subscribe to the notion that there must have been one group of wealthy elites who invented the religious beliefs in a civilization and foisted them onto the ignorant masses in order to oppress them and preserve the status quo. Though these ideas have the semblance of a critical theory, this scenario cannot simply be projected onto any religion as a substitute for studying a society and culture. Students who take this approach often deduce specific social realities (e.g. forms of oppression that are, or must have been, occurring) from the general beliefs of the religion instead of finding evidence that shows how things actually were (usually Buddhism and Hinduism are picked on, for reasons I cannot fathom). When actual information exists, there is no justification for resorting to hypotheses and deductions.

Form

Closely related to content, and nearly as important, is the written expression of your thoughts. If your ideas are not clear on the page, they are not clear in your head either. Any university expects all of its students to be able to write proficiently in the language of instruction. For some students this means consulting a tutor in a writing lab or taking a course on effective writing. People rarely discern the rules of grammar and punctuation inductively by reading and writing. These things must be explained and therefore learned from a style manual or a writing instructor. The time you spend learning the rules will be nothing compared with the time you will save in wondering why your sentences look wrong. Studying a style manual will allow you not only to write better and faster but also to think more clearly. These abilities will be every bit as useful to you as the specific knowledge you acquire through writing papers. (Essay structure and style will be discussed below.)

Since there is no one right way to evaluate an essay, the actual breakdown of your mark will depend on the predilections of the individual grader. This is the marking scheme that I use:

Content:	50%
Evidence of research:	10%
Structure and organization:	10%
Independent thought:	10%
Style, grammar, and spelling:	15%
Documentation:	05%

How to Write an Essay

When to Start

For people who start their research a month or so early, and work at their leisure two or three afternoons a week, essay writing can be quite rewarding. It is to the people who habitually start their essays within a week of the due date that essays seem like massive undertakings. Essay writing deprives them not only of all their spare time but also of their sleep, and every other thing they have to do that week becomes a crisis. Should some unanticipated circumstance prevent them from finishing on time they begin to feel that someone up there hates them. And when they fail the paper because they have not done nearly enough work, they marvel, 'But I never worked so hard in my life!' (I can safely assume that the people who start the night before will not be reading this book.)

Those 'acts of God' that beset you the week an essay is due may seem to be unavoidable and, therefore, excuses. But your more enlightened grader may interpret these occurrences as omens warning you to repent of your procrastinating ways. Remember, you know as early as the beginning of the course what assignments you have to do. Disdain for writing essays is probably the main thing keeping you from starting early; and that disdain is probably the result of the negative experiences associated with starting late.

What to Read

Extensive research into your specific topic is what enables you to draw independent conclusions. Usually a few hundred (yes, hundred) pages of reading is required – and expected – in addition to the relevant chapters of the course textbook. General discussions of a religion that you get from a textbook and from other general reference works such as handbooks and encyclopedias give you an essential foundational knowledge about that tradition and some protection against making obvious mistakes. The bulk of your reading, however, must be in books and articles written about your specific topic. Those works present enough of the evidence to permit you to do an adequate analysis. The specific information you need is available at the university libraries. The problem is finding it.

Locating Scholarly Literature

If you are having trouble finding a topic, browse the stacks for interesting books. When you have a specific topic, a subject or keyword search in the online catalogue can get you started. There is a trick to this, however, for you are bound to have trouble figuring out what words to type into the search box for books on your specific subject. If your subject is, for instance, tenth-century Jewish manuscripts, what do you type into the search box? Is it 'tenth-century Jewish manuscripts' or 'Jewish manuscripts, tenth-century' or 'manuscripts, Jewish, tenth-century' or something else? The chances of guessing correctly are a bit better than your odds of winning big at a nickel slot machine. But once you find one book that addresses your subject, you can find out from its online catalogue record what subjects it was catalogued under. With some luck, the subject listing that you are looking for will be there. If not, you can attempt a more general keyword search, say for 'Jewish manuscripts', and then scroll through the list until you find some books that look promising. Check how those books are categorized by subject headings. Eventually, you should find the headings that will bring you directly to the books you want.

Once you have located one or two good books or articles on your subject, search their notes and bibliographies for other items of primary or secondary literature that appear to be relevant to your topic. Then locate those materials. Repeat this process with those additional materials until you have enough literature to work with. Be prepared to make two or three trips to the library. It is better to start with fairly recent books and articles, since the bibliographies they contain will be more up to date. Consider examining recent doctoral dissertations on your subject. Although you might not understand the dissertations themselves, they should contain the most complete bibliographies of secondary literature. Find out if your library allows you to search for and download doctoral dissertations as electronic files.

Avoid really old secondary literature unless you are studying the history of scholarship on a topic. Occasionally, a student submits a paper that is based largely on scholarship that is a century old. More often than not, these secondary sources are books whose copyright has expired, allowing some industrious persons to convert them into electronic format and post them on the internet. Very old books are not going to tell you what scholars think about your subject today. Often enough, what seemed like a brilliant idea a century ago seemed passé twenty years later, then became quaint around the time your parents were born, and passed into astonishing naïveté during your elementary-school years. Today we would file those ideas under What Were They Thinking?

Older Western scholarship on Middle Eastern and Asian religions is sometimes laden with cultural stereotypes. Earlier scholars were more prone to generalize about 'the Orient' and 'the Oriental', as if everyone in Asia and the Middle East shared a common mentality.[1] Even as recently as the 1960s many scholars supposed that language systems constrained thought in fundamental ways such that one could contrast the Greek mind with the Hebrew. More recent scholarship is highly sceptical of generalizations applied over vast areas and numerous cultures and recognizes that it is better to focus on particular cultures.

Just as older studies have their problems and limitations, so too do older translations of primary sources. Admittedly, in some cases the most recent translations of ancient texts are a century old, and they can still be used with profit, but you should try to use more recent translations if they exist, assuming that they were produced by competent translators. More up-to-date scholarly translations will utilize not only any subsequent research that has been published on that ancient text but also any additional manuscripts that have since been discovered. And the parlance will be more contemporary.

Using up-to-date translations is especially important for the Bible. Our modern Bibles are actually based on thousands of different manuscripts, no two of which are identical. Indeed, there are more textual variants in the manuscripts of the New Testament than there are words in the New Testament. The job of collating those manuscripts and determining the best reading wherever textual variants occur has become an extraordinarily complex enterprise, with the consequence that professional textual critics are forever revising their reconstructions of the original wording of the Bible, taking newly discovered manuscripts and the latest research into consideration. Usually these revisions involve a word or phrase here and there, but you might be very surprised to learn that some verses of the Bible are no longer included in the best modern versions because those verses are absent from the oldest manuscripts and appear to be the work of later scribes.

So definitely avoid out-of-date translations such as the King James Bible. Yet keep in mind that relatively new translations are not always more reliable. You can figure out which translations of an ancient text are most reliable by noting what the experts themselves use. Most New Testament scholars, for instance, use the Revised Standard Version, the New Revised Standard Version, the New International Version, and the Jerusalem Bible. Those translations were put together by international teams of respected scholars. By contrast, many popular contemporary translations of scriptures are not sufficiently accurate or literal for the purposes of scholarship. Translations aimed at potential converts or at people who peruse the religion and spirituality sections of popular bookstores are generally intended to make a text more accessible to the uninitiated reader by diminishing its obscurity and complexity. These books generally offer not so much a literal translation as a paraphrase of what the translator thinks it means. Christian examples include: The Living Bible; Holy Bible, New Living Translation; and the Good News Bible. What you need is a highly literal scholarly translation that you can interpret for yourself.

You can also find good translations of individual books of scripture in some academic commentaries on those texts. For nearly every religious text there is at least one scholar who has studied it for a decade or more. Any translation and commentary produced by such a person is indispensable.

Be highly sceptical about the notes and introductions that appear in devotional study editions of the Bible, the Qur'an, the Bhagavad-Gita (e.g. Prabhupada's), and other scriptures, including the annotations that accompany the best scholarly translations. The people who write the annotations are usually hired by the publisher and are not necessarily connected to the body of scholars who made the translation. Although the notes in study editions may sound authoritative and purely factual, with few exceptions their purpose is not academic but doctrinal: they offer explanations and clarifications that accord with the theology of the religious community that published that study edition.

Journal articles and other publications on all aspects of religion are catalogued by subject in a yearly periodical called the *Religion Index One* (also available on CD-ROM). There is also a *Religion Index Two*, which catalogues chapters in multi-author books, and an *Index to Book Reviews in Religion*. These three resources have been combined in the online resource *ATLA Index*. Again, when using the print editions of these indexes you might want to start from the most recent volume and work backwards.

Also indispensable is *JSTOR* (*Journal Storage*), a digital archive of scholarly journals in the form of scanned images. This resource allows patrons not only to search the contents of archived journals for articles containing particular words and phrases but also to read and download those articles as electronic image files. The internet search engine Google has a similar resource for searching the contents of books, called Google Book Search. *JSTOR* and Google Book Search make it much easier to find overlooked discussions of obscure topics.

There are also more specialized online indexes for religions. Students of Islam and the Muslim world have the *Index Islamicus*. *Index theologicus* indexes articles in theological journals and essays in some books from 1984 onwards. It is not as complete as *ATLA* but keeps more current, being updated daily. EBSCO Information Services provides biblical scholars with several online indexes: *Catholic Periodical and Literature Index*, *Index to Jewish Periodicals*, *New Testament Abstracts* and *Old Testament Abstracts* – all combined with *ATLA* into one search engine. *Religious and Theological*

Abstracts offers brief summaries of articles. Scholars of Judaism use *Jewish Abstracts* and *RAMBI: Index of Articles on Jewish Studies*. The *Bibliography of Asian Studies* indexes articles in the one hundred journals most used in Asian Studies. See the Select Bibliography at the end of this guide for additional indexes and bibliographies in print format.

Since you are not writing a religious essay, you must not get your information about a religion from devotional or sectarian literature, for example books available at religious bookstores (or the religion sections of commercial book-stores) but not found on the shelves of the university libraries. The authors you consult should be experts in *the academic study* of religion (usually persons employed as lecturers in accredited universities) rather than experts in the practice of religion (e.g. gurus, saints, celebrities, theologians – unless these persons are also respected academics). Scholarly books are not spiritually edifying. If an author is brimming with adulation for the religion, or pauses to draw life lessons for the believer, the chances are good that she or he is not also offering an impartial academic analysis. Not every book written by a scholar qualifies as academic and impartial. Some scholars occasionally write theological or spiritual works intended for believers, and in the process combine academic and religious presuppositions in a way that can be confusing to people new to the academic study of religion. Other authors are apologists who strive to defend traditional beliefs by disputing 'secular' scholarship on its own terms. Apologetic and pseudo-scholarly books are sometimes donated to university libraries by religious organizations in an effort to disseminate their views.

It is up to you to discern the biases of the authors you consult and to use appropriate scholarly research. Often (though not always) the title of a book will give some indication of the kind of work contained within. A book with a title like *Living and Loving with Krishna* is unlikely to be scholarly. A book with a title like *Buddhism and the State in Sixteenth-Century Japan* is unlikely to be pious. Good publishers use a process of anonymous peer review to determine which books and articles merit publication. Two or more reviewers are selected on the basis of their expertise to determine whether a manuscript deserves to be published. The identity of the author is withheld from the reviewers, and the identities of the reviewers are withheld from the author. This process is even more reliable when the person who decides which manuscripts merit reviewing is also an expert in that field. Hence books published in a series edited by a respected scholar are nearly always highly competent.[2]

Essays posted on the internet are a mixed bag. Ones published online in peer-reviewed academic journals are as reliable as their print counterparts. Essays posted by university instructors on their course web pages are much more likely to be scholarly than essays and blogs posted by amateurs, which should always be ignored. So much unreliable information exists on the internet that some professors object to students using any internet sources that are not peer-reviewed or also published in print formats. Public libraries can be just as unreliable places to find scholarship.

If you are in doubt about a writer's academic credentials, you can check the name in one of the online religion indexes (e.g. *ATLA Index* and *JSTOR*) to see if he or she has published any articles or books that can be found in university libraries. You can quickly get a sense of a scholar's status and reputation by skimming the reviews of that person's books archived in *JSTOR*. As James R. Kennedy pointed out, scholars who have published several 'favorably reviewed' books on your subject deserve more of your trust and attention than those who have never published on the subject before, whereas scholars 'whose only other publication was in an altogether different field' deserve your profound scepticism.[3] Consider consulting with your professor (or grader) about the research materials you have found. Part 4 (below) describes in detail the hallmarks of bad scholarship.

Beginning to Write

Do not start writing until you have some opinion on the right solution to the issue you are confronting. Otherwise you might produce a paper that wanders aimlessly through the evidence, never reaching a conclusion. Wait until you have an idea of what you want to argue, and then start writing down (or typing out) these arguments. If you have done extensive research you could probably fill up ten pages in an evening. But when you read them the next day, those pages will probably seem pretty awful. Treat them as a first draft. Unless you are incredibly bright, you probably need to 'see' your ideas on paper before you can adequately evaluate them. Having your arguments set out in writing enables you to critique them as if you were someone else, someone who knows the same things you do but is not partial to your interpretation. Ask yourself: Are your arguments logical? Do they suffice to establish that your perspective is better than all the others? Once you detect the weaknesses in your arguments you will be led to explore new ideas that would not have occurred to you before you started writing. You will probably come to change some of your initial views.

Writing and Rewriting

As you refine your arguments, your thesis will become clearer in your mind. Nearer the end of your work you will know precisely what you are succeeding in arguing, and for that reason you should put off writing your opening paragraph until you have finished the body of the essay. It is through the process of writing and revising that you work out your precise thesis. The thoughts you had while researching your essay will have been somewhat random and scattered – as ordinary thinking usually is. The process of writing is what allows you to systematically structure these disjoined insights. Thinking 'on paper' permits a degree of clarity you could not obtain otherwise.

Always work your thoughts into distinct paragraphs, each developing a particular idea. If your paragraphs tend to be only a few sentences long or else go on for a few pages, you have not refined your thoughts to the point of clarity. It will take some time for you to grasp what you are trying to say, but when you reach that point you will be able to order your ideas into a logical sequence of arguments that support your thesis. Throughout the process of rewriting, periodically print a draft of the essay and make corrections on the pages themselves. It is much easier to get a sense of the whole argument when you can see all of it on paper. You might want to subdivide your essay using subheadings. If you do, make sure that everything beneath a heading actually belongs to that topic and that all second- or third-level subdivisions belong within their respective higher-level topics.

Your introductory paragraph should be as concise as you can make it. There is no need for lengthy preamble (or padding). Outline the basic issue as tersely as possible, and then clearly and overtly state your thesis, mentioning how you will go about demonstrating your case. Always strive for clarity. By the end of the first few paragraphs, your reader should have a clear basic understanding of what you intend to accomplish and how you intend to do it. Half a page may be all you need for the introduction. Use the introductions in published articles as a model.

Once your argument is complete, the essay may be concluded with a summary of what you demonstrated and some comments on the relevance (academic or social) of this research. Resist the urge to slip out of the academic mode. This is not the place to add your two cents' worth. Do not get personal or emotional or sermonize or castigate or prescribe solutions to the problems of the religious groups you investigated. Just remind your reader of what you have contributed to the academic enterprise and, if you wish, note how your conclusions can be useful to those who, in a different context, strive to improve the world.

Proofreading

Once you consider the essay finished, you should slowly and carefully read through a printout of the entire paper, looking for mistakes in spelling and grammar. Mistakes that are easily missed when looking at a computer screen are more easily spotted in print. Common mistakes include subject–verb and subject–pronoun disagreements (e.g. using plural pronouns for singular nouns or the reverse), ambiguous pronouns, missing antecedents, missing periods, missing closing quotation marks or closing parentheses, inconsistent use of tenses, changes in font (resulting from copying words from another electronic document, such as a religious text or online library catalogue, into your essay), incorrect punctuation (such as using a hyphen instead of a dash), inconsistent punctuation (such as forming dashes in more than one way), inconsistent use of American and British stylistic conventions, and wrong words (e.g. *their* instead of *there*). You will rarely catch these kinds of errors and inconsistencies by reading at your normal speed. At your normal speed, you see the words you expect to see, which are the words you remember typing. Therefore at the proofreading stage you need to read slowly enough that the syllables of words register in your mind, but not so slowly that you lose the train of thought.

As you enter your final corrections into your word processor, you are liable to make new errors, so I advise rereading each sentence that you modify, to make sure that you have not substituted one error for another. The very last thing you should do before printing your final copy is run the spell checker a final time, in case you misspelled something in the changes you made. Always scan through your final printout for problems in the layout that resulted from your final revisions. Sometimes titles get shifted to the last line on a page or line breaks mysteriously appear before the end of a line.

Quotations

Quote sparingly. You are not doing your own work if your essay is a patchwork of quotations. Heavy reliance on other people's wording suggests that you have not fully digested and synthesized these ideas. You best convey your grasp of these ideas by relating them in your own words (with proper documentation, of course). There are, however, times when quotations are better than paraphrases. If the exact wording of the author's statement is important to the point you are making, or if the author's opinion might seem incredible to your reader, then use a quotation to demonstrate that you are not misrepresenting that person's opinion. Likewise, the rhetorical effect of quoting an authority is a reasonable way of persuading your readers of an uncontroversial point of minor significance to your paper when you anticipate that your readers might find this point surprising (if they still have doubts, they can examine the work from which you quoted). You might also wish to 'quote when an author clearly says something better than you could, or when it is said in a clearly memorable way', as Gordon D. Fee so ably stated (well, perhaps I could have said this in my own words just as ably).[4] Admittedly, it is sometimes difficult to say the same thing in your own words because the author's wording was the most natural (that is my excuse for the previous quotation). And there is nothing wrong with reusing a few choice words and apt phrases. In cases where you do use some of the author's phrasing out of necessity or preference, you should either quote the author's statement in full or incorporate the borrowed phrases as short quotations within your own paraphrase. Paraphrases that use some of the author's phrases without quotation marks around them are called illegitimate paraphrases and constitute a minor form of plagiarism. So be careful.

As I indicate in my discussion of fallacies, quotations of scholars do not prove points or effectively substantiate your arguments. Many students think that a position is established by quoting a real scholar who expresses that opinion. But unless a quotation includes an assessment of the evidence, it really only demonstrates that this particular scholar holds that opinion. Even renowned authorities can be wrong. (Scholars must often be wrong considering how much they disagree with each other.) It is up to you to argue the significant or essential points you make in your paper *by discussing the evidence*. If the books you are using do not relate this evidence, they are probably too general for your purposes.

As soon as you add a quotation to your essay, check it for copying mistakes. If the sentences you are quoting contain unusual spellings or mistakes, indicate your awareness of these problems by inserting the Latin word *sic* (meaning 'thus') in brackets. You may silently correct obvious typos in the source. Use brackets to insert your own comments or clarification into a quotation. Though the temptation can be strong, avoid using brackets to interject your scorn for the stupidity of another writer (e.g., adding '[!]' or '[*sic*]' after a particularly foolish comment). These interjections insult your readers' intelligence by implying that they need cues to recognize stupidity, and undermine your own objectivity by suggesting that you want your readers to think little of this scholar.

Do not put your quotations in italics. Students sometimes do this because they see italicized quotations (called epigraphs) at the heads of chapters, but that is the only place where it is proper to italicize a quotation. If the material you are citing is already completely in italics, put it in normal type, but in your documentation add in parentheses 'italics removed'. You are free to italicize words that you want to emphasize in your quotation, provided you add a notation such as 'italics mine' or 'emphasis added' in parentheses. If, on the other hand, you are concerned that your reader might suppose that you italicized the words that are important to your point when in fact they were already italicized in your source, put 'italics original' in parentheses.

Block Quotations

Quotations longer than a hundred words are set as block quotations. These are indented from the left margin (or both margins), single-spaced (or a spacing between single and double), usually set in type one font size smaller than the surrounding type, and set off from the body of the paragraph by a triple line-space before and after the quotation. The quotation itself is *not* put in quotation marks; the block format serves as the indication that the words are being quoted. Quotation marks appear within block quotations only when the quoted material itself includes quotations or direct speech. If you use a word processor, a simple way to determine the length of your quotation is by highlighting the quoted words and selecting the word-count feature.

Quotations briefer than one hundred words may also be set in block format if they are important enough to the discussion to be worth highlighting. For example, if you keep referring to a verse of scripture over the course of a few pages you might want to set it apart in this fashion to facilitate your reader's inspection. (See the section 'Style' for discussion of the punctuation preceding quotations and the proper use of ellipsis points.)

Documentation

Some graders read the bibliography of an essay first, so that the body of the essay is fresh in their minds when they start working out the grade. The students who guess at how to format a footnote or a bibliography entry, or rely entirely on faulty memory, make a terrible first impression on these graders, or a very bad last impression on the ones who read the bibliography just before they work out the grade. Graders are baffled by incorrectly formatted documentation because the books and articles that their students are documenting normally contain correctly formatted notes and bibliographies, and students usually have these items open before them as they copy down the bibliographical information; they *could* find out the proper format with relative ease, but they somehow miss an opportunity to bias their grader in a positive way with flawless documentation.

What Is Documented?

Some people suppose that notes are required only when directly quoting someone. Documentation is actually required whenever you make use of someone else's ideas, even if you use your own words to express them. Every time you rely on another writer's idea or way of describing a matter, you must note your intellectual debt. That is not to say that you always need to specify the source from which you learned something. Information that is common knowledge *to scholars within your chosen subject area* and information that you have come across in more than one item of secondary literature does not need to be attributed to any one author. If, however, you suspect that your reader might want to verify a particular point, or learn more about it, by all means add a footnote. An over-documented essay gives the impression that you did not read enough to know that much of the information you are citing is actually common knowledge within that field, whereas an under-documented essay gives the impression that you need to pretend that you are capable of thinking for yourself (and gets you in trouble). A properly documented essay will accurately convey the full extent of your research.

Avoiding Plagiarism

Plagiarism is the academic offence of presenting another person's words or ideas as one's own. Students commit plagiarism when they submit another person's essay, have someone write an essay for them, or lift sentences and paragraphs (not to mention complete chapters or articles) from the scholarship they used. They are similarly cheating when they resubmit work they did for another course. The penalties for these offences are stern, and may include expulsion from the college or an automatic course mark of zero with the word *plagiarism* appearing beside it on transcripts. The severity of the penalty depends on the weight of the assignment and the extent to which the work submitted is not one's own. There is no need to fret about whether to put quotation marks around commonplace conjunctions of words or standard phrases that appear in your sources – these are the building blocks of thought, not anyone's intellectual property. And there is nothing wrong with writing a new and essentially different essay on a topic you previously researched (unless your instructor asked you to write on a new topic).

The internet has made plagiarism much more convenient, but also much easier to catch. No matter how arduous it was to find an essay on the internet, a suspicious grader needs only to type a distinctive phrase from the essay into a search engine to be taken there directly. Purchased essays may also be readily traceable, for they may have been sold to other students who took the course, taken from the internet, plagiarized from published sources, or stolen from the pile of essays that were returned the previous year. 'Original' plagiarized essays that incorporate passages from various sources invariably contain sections and 'seams' where the plagiarist's inferior understanding and writing style are clearly discernible. Expensive made-to-order essays, on the other hand, are commissioned from people who write 'professionally' and are vastly more knowledgeable than the student. If a grader is curious to know whether a student has the knowledge to write a particular paper, it takes only a casual conversation to find that out: 'Great essay, Harold. Really engrossing. By the way, could you explain to me what you mean by the term defocalization?' A simple question like that can let the grader know whether plagiarism is worth investigating. And if Harold truly does not understand his own essay, what tribunal is going to conclude that he wrote it? Catching plagiarism is not as difficult as it might seem.

Methods of Documentation

The method of documentation you choose should be appropriate for the type of essay you are writing. If you have few references you might want to use the author–date method, which places the documentation within the body of the essay inside parentheses that contain the author's surname, the year of publication, and the page range. The full publication information for each work appears only at the end, in the bibliography (*The Chicago Manual of Style* calls it a reference list). Note, though, that this in-text method may incline you to document too sparingly (in effect, to plagiarize), for the inclusion of many parenthetical references within the body of an essay can seem obtrusive. If you have many references and periodically wish to add supplementary information, use notes (footnotes or endnotes).

Notes remain the most common method of documentation in Religious Studies scholarship. The superscript number in the body of the essay (referred to as the note callout) unobtrusively indicates the existence of documentary or supplementary information without compelling the reader to consider it. More important, notes provide a place for additional evidence or relevant digressions that are hard to fit into the body of the essay. You might find that in the course of substantiating the main points of your essay, you need to make brief assertions about peripheral matters related to these points. You can deal with these peripheral matters summarily in notes by citing the conclusions of authors who, in your view, adequately examined these issues. Although the note method is sufficient by itself, some authors supplement parenthetical references with explanatory footnotes.

Notes and Bibliographies

Books called style manuals establish and explain the conventions for arranging bibliographical information in notes and bibliographies. Two of the most influential manuals are the *MLA Handbook for Writers of Research Papers* and *The*

Chicago Manual of Style. You can find these books in the reference section of any college library. University bookstores usually carry less technical books on writing and style based on the standard reference books; the better ones are worth buying and reading completely. Many useful but brief style guides exist on the internet. The locations of the guides change periodically, but typing 'MLA style guide' or 'Chicago Manual of Style' into a search engine should lead you to them. Conventions for citing internet and multimedia resources (e.g. CD-ROMs, essays posted on the World Wide Web, electronic mailing lists, and e-mail correspondence) appear in the most recent editions of the major style manuals. For a more comprehensive treatment, see Janice R. Walker and Todd Taylor, *The Columbia Guide to Online Style* (New York: Columbia University Press, 2006).

Footnotes are single-spaced and one font size smaller than the font used for the body of the essay. By contrast, endnotes are double-spaced and in the same font size as the essay. The first line of a note is indented, similar to a paragraph. The number of the note does not need to be in superscript (set above the line), though its corresponding number within the body of the essay (the call-out) should be. Unlike the bibliography format, the author's first name comes first in a note. When documenting books, the *city* of publication must be named. It goes *before* the publisher (add the province, country, or state only if the city is obscure or if it is likely to be confused with a better-known city of the same name). Because notes are sentences, they conclude with terminal punctuation. Even brief citations of secondary literature must conclude with a period (or, *conceivably*, a question mark or an exclamation mark).

Subtitles are introduced by colons. When the title ends in a question mark or exclamation mark, use that punctuation mark instead of a colon (not both together). You may choose, as a rule, not to include subtitles or series titles in the notes, though sometimes the subtitle is worth mentioning if the title of the book is not self-explanatory (do include subtitles and series titles in the bibliography).

Italicize the titles of works that stand on their own: books, journals, magazines, plays, movies, television series (not individual episodes), and major works of music (e.g. symphonies and tone poems). Although you might see book titles underlined in some secondary literature and in academic writing guides created in the era of the typewriter, underlining is merely a substitute for italics when italics are not available. If a title that you need to italicize already contains italicized words, such as the title of another book, set those italicized words in regular or non-italicized type (called roman type) to distinguish them from the other words in the title.

Set in quotation marks the titles of long unpublished works, such as book manuscripts and dissertations, and short works that are part of something larger: articles, essays, chapters, sections of books, titled reviews, titled interviews, short stories, poems, songs and tracks on an album, and episodes of a television series. The title remains in roman type except where it contains italicized words. If the title already contains words in quotation marks, the rule for quotations within quotations applies: if you follow the American convention and use double quotation marks for quotations, then put (or keep) the already quoted words in single quotation marks; if you follow the British convention and use single quotation marks for quotations, then make sure that the already quoted words are in double quotation marks. All of the major religions teach that it is a sin to put all titles in both italics and quotation marks. (See the section 'Style' for the capitalization of titles and the placement of punctuation.)

In Religious Studies, notes and their corresponding call-outs must be numbered consecutively (that is, the call-outs do not refer to numbered items in the bibliography). If possible, place the note call-outs at the ends of the sentences they document. If the note documents something early in a sentence, but not what comes later, it is best to put the call-out immediately after the statement with which it is associated, preferably after a comma or semicolon if there is one, or to explain in the note what it documents.

You only need to give the full publication information about a book or article the first time you cite it (and again in the bibliography). Scholars once used the words **op. cit.** ('in the cited work') and **loc. cit.** ('in the place cited') to refer readers to the first or last citation of a work, respectively, but this approach aggravates the reader, who has to search back through the notes to find the one that contains the work's title. Thus it is now common for subsequent references to mention the author's surname, a shortened title of a few *consecutive* words that summarize the work's essence, and the page or page range (see 'The Standard Format for References', below, for examples).

There is no need to give any publication information when citing a well-known standard translation of a religion's scriptures, such as a version of the Bible, or to list this translation in the bibliography. Just mention the translation you are using in a note at the beginning of the essay or after the first direct quotation (e.g. 'All quotations from the Bible are from the Revised Standard Version'). If you use more than one translation, qualify this statement (e.g. 'Except where indicated, all quotations . . .') and note the exceptions in the parentheses following the quotation (e.g. Exod. 21:7–8; New International Version). You may use the standard abbreviations for these versions (e.g. RSV and NIV) if your grader is likely to know them. Note that there is no point mentioning a particular translation *unless you actually quote from it*. Likewise, there is no benefit in giving page numbers in addition to scriptural references *unless you are quoting infrequently from a non-standard translation*. The difference has to do with accessibility. Well-known standard translations are sold by a variety of publishers in a variety of formats, each with its own pagination. Your reader will probably find it easier to obtain a standard translation in a format other than the one you used, so it is pointless to give page numbers in addition to parenthetical scriptural references. On the other hand, non-standard translations, such as original translations that appear in scholarly commentaries, are available in only one or two formats, so a reader who wants to check your quotation will likely decide to examine the same book from which you are quoting; you should therefore list that work in your bibliography. Whether you give the page numbers depends on whether this will help your reader. Certainly if you quote from a non-standard translation only occasionally, you should attach a reference with page numbers to each citation. But if this translation is your principal source and you cite it frequently, it is sufficient to give a general acknowledgement such as 'All quotations from the Maitri Upanishad are from . . .', then document the book, indicating where the translation appears within it (unless it is spread throughout the commentary).

Unlike notes, items in the bibliography are not numbered and are listed in alphabetical order according to the (principal) authors' surnames. The indenting of bibliography items is the reverse of that used for notes (i.e. hanging indents). The specific pages you referred to in your essay are not mentioned in the bibliography. Include only the inclusive pages of writings that are embedded in larger works (e.g. journal articles, book reviews, forewords by someone other than the book's author, and chapters or essays published in multi-author books or in collections of essays by a single author). When the bibliography contains more than one work by either the same person or the *exact* same collaboration of persons, the full name or names are not repeated but replaced by lines made either of three em-dashes (———), for the American style, or two em-dashes (——), for British style.

If you are confused by the way that publication information is presented on the title page of the book, or forgot to record some of this information before you returned the book, you may be able to get the information you need through the university library's online catalogue. That will save you having to find the book again.

The Standard Format for References

What follow are examples of documentation that conform to the conventions of *The Chicago Manual of Style*, displaying the note format followed by the bibliography format. I use Chicago's convention of denoting endnotes and footnotes with the letter N, and bibliography entries with the letter B. Since Chicago is an American manual, my examples will use American punctuation. However, at the end of this section I will explain the punctuation changes under British style.

Printed Secondary Literature

BOOKS WITH ONE AUTHOR

N: 1. George D. Chryssides, *Exploring New Religions* (London and New York: Cassell, 1999), 140–41.

B: Chryssides, George D. *Exploring New Religions*. London and New York: Cassell, 1999.

BOOKS WITH TWO OR THREE AUTHORS, TRANSLATORS, OR EDITORS

N: 2. Howard Eilberg-Schwartz and Wendy Doniger, eds., *Off with Her Head! The Denial of Women's Identity in Myth, Religion, and Culture* (Berkeley: University of California Press, 1995), 28.

B: Eilberg-Schwartz, Howard, and Wendy Doniger, eds. *Off with Her Head! The Denial of Women's Identity in Myth, Religion, and Culture*. Berkeley: University of California Press, 1995.

BOOKS WITH MORE THAN THREE AUTHORS, TRANSLATORS, OR EDITORS

N: 3. Henri Frankfort et al., *The Intellectual Adventure of Ancient Man: An Essay on Speculative Thought in the Ancient Near East* (Chicago: University of Chicago Press, 1946), 157.

B: Frankfort, Henri, Henriette A. Frankfort, John A.
     Wilson, Thorkild Jacobsen, and William A. Irwin.
     *The Intellectual Adventure of Ancient Man: An Essay on
     Speculative Thought in the Ancient Near East*. Chicago:
     University of Chicago Press, 1946.

N: 4. Willi Marxsen, *Mark the Evangelist: Studies on the
     Redaction History of the Gospel*, trans. James Boyce et al.
     (Nashville: Abingdon, 1969), 100.

B: Marxsen, Willi. *Mark the Evangelist: Studies on the
     Redaction History of the Gospel*. Translated by James
     Boyce, Donald Juel, William Poehlmann, with Roy
     A. Harrisville. Nashville: Abingdon, 1969.

The Latin words 'et al.' may be replaced with their English
equivalent 'and others'.

BOOKS WITH A CORPORATE AUTHOR OR PREPARED BY A
COMMITTEE

N: 5. The Jesus Seminar, *The Once and Future Jesus* (Santa
     Rosa, CA: Polebridge, 2000), 150.

B: The Jesus Seminar. *The Once and Future Jesus*. Santa
     Rosa, CA: Polebridge, 2000.

In the bibliography, this book would be alphabetized under
Jesus.

BOOKS WITH ONE EDITOR

N: 6. Willard G. Oxtoby, ed., *World Religions: Eastern
     Traditions*, 2nd ed. (Don Mills, ON: Oxford University
     Press, 2002), 298.

B: Oxtoby, Willard G., ed. *World Religions: Eastern Tradi-
     tions*. 2nd ed. Don Mills, ON: Oxford University
     Press, 2002.

BOOKS WITH TWO EDITORS

N: 7. George D. Chryssides and Margaret Z. Wilkins,
     eds., *A Reader in New Religious Movements* (London and
     New York: Continuum, 2006), 69.

B: Chryssides, George D., and Margaret Z. Wilkins, eds. *A Reader in New Religious Movements*. London and New York: Continuum, 2006.

This format is for citing an entire book. If you are citing a particular essay or chapter in a multi-author book, see 'ESSAYS OR CHAPTERS IN A MULTI-AUTHOR BOOK'.

BOOKS WITH THEIR OWN TITLE IN A MULTI-VOLUME WORK WITH A SEPARATE TITLE

N: 8. Raymond E. Brown, *From Gethsemane to the Grave*, vol. 1 of *The Death of the Messiah: A Commentary on the Passion Narratives in the Four Gospels*, Anchor Bible Reference Library (New York: Doubleday, 1994), 387.

B: Brown, Raymond E. *From Gethsemane to the Grave*. Vol. 1 of *The Death of the Messiah: A Commentary on the Passion Narratives in the Four Gospels*. Anchor Bible Reference Library. New York: Doubleday, 1994.

The first title is the title of the individual book; the second title is the title of the multi-volume work.

PARTICULAR VOLUMES IN A MULTI-VOLUME WORK WITH ONE TITLE

N: 9. William Theodore de Bary, ed., *Sources of Chinese Tradition* (New York: Columbia University Press, 1960), 1:34–47.

B: de Bary, William Theodore, ed. *Sources of Chinese Tradition*. 2 vols. New York: Columbia University Press, 1960.

In the note, the volume number precedes the page number(s), separated by a colon. The total number of volumes is not mentioned in the note, but is mentioned in the bibliography entry.

N: 10. Arthur P. Wolf, "Gods, Ghosts and Ancestors," in *Religion and Ritual in Chinese Society*, ed. Arthur P. Wolf, Studies in Chinese Society (Stanford: Stanford University Press, 1974), 131–82.

B: Wolf, Arthur P. "Gods, Ghosts and Ancestors." In *Religion and Ritual in Chinese Society*, edited by Arthur P. Wolf, 131–82. Studies in Chinese Society. Stanford: Stanford University Press, 1974.

A subsequent first reference to a different essay from the same book need not reproduce all of the bibliographical information (later references using a shortened title will omit the editor and book title):

N: 11. Jack Potter, "Cantonese Shamanism," in Wolf, ed., *Religion and Ritual*, 210.

B: Potter, Jack. "Cantonese Shamanism." In *Religion and Ritual in Chinese Society*, edited by Arthur P. Wolf, 207–31. Studies in Chinese Society. Stanford: Stanford University Press, 1974.

Note that in bibliography entries, if the editor is associated with the book as a whole and not exclusively with the part of the book being cited (as when citing a foreword or afterword written by someone other than the author, or an essay in a volume compiled by the editor), a comma is used to attach the words 'edited by' more closely to the title of the book. When there is no possibility of confusion over the editor's role in relation to the book (as when the book has only one author and one editor), the editor's name is separated from the book by a period.

N: 12. Ninian Smart, foreword to *Religious Studies and the Nuclear Age*, ed. Ira Chernus and Edward Tabor

Linenthal (Albany: State University of New York Press, 1989), ix–x.

B: Smart, Ninian. Foreword to *Religious Studies and the Nuclear Age*, edited by Ira Chernus and Edward Tabor Linenthal, ix–x. Albany: State University of New York Press, 1989.

N: 13. Arthur Darby Nock, foreword to *Greek Folk Religion*, by Martin P. Nilsson (New York: Harper, 1961), xiii–xv.

B: Nock, Arthur Darby. Foreword to *Greek Folk Religion*, by Martin P. Nilsson, xiii–xv. New York: Harper, 1961.

BOOK REVIEWS

N: 14. Russell T. McCutcheon, review of *Savage Systems: Colonialism and Comparative Religion in Southern Africa*, by David Chidester, *History of Religions* 39 (1999): 73–76.

B: McCutcheon, Russell T. Review of *Savage Systems: Colonialism and Comparative Religion in Southern Africa*, by David Chidester. *History of Religions* 39 (1999): 73–76.

UNREVISED BOOKS REPRINTED BY THE SAME PUBLISHER

N: 15. Edward Conze, trans., *Buddhist Scriptures*, Penguin Classics (1959; repr., Harmondsworth, England: Penguin, 1969), 85.

B: Conze, Edward, trans. *Buddhist Scriptures*. Penguin Classics. 1959. Reprint, Harmondsworth, England: Penguin, 1969.

UNREVISED BOOKS REPRINTED BY A DIFFERENT PUBLISHER

N: 16. Morton Smith and R. Joseph Hoffman, eds., *What the Bible Really Says* (Buffalo: Prometheus Books, 1989; San Francisco: HarperSanFrancisco, 1993), 82.

B: Smith, Morton, and R. Joseph Hoffman, eds. *What the Bible Really Says*. San Francisco: HarperSanFrancisco, 1993. First published 1989 by Prometheus Books.

REVISED BOOKS REPUBLISHED BY A DIFFERENT PUBLISHER

N: 17. Mircea Eliade, *The Myth of the Eternal Return: Cosmos and History*, trans. Willard R. Trask, with a new introduction by Jonathan Z. Smith, Bollingen Series 46, 2nd pbk. ed. (New York: Pantheon Books, 1954; Princeton: Princeton University Press, 2005), 93.

B: Eliade, Mircea. *The Myth of the Eternal Return: Cosmos and History*. Translated by Willard R. Trask. Bollingen Series 46. New York: Pantheon Books, 1954. Reprinted with a new introduction by Jonathan Z. Smith. 2nd pbk. ed. Princeton: Princeton University Press, 2005.

UNPUBLISHED DISSERTATIONS

N: 18. Terry Tak-ling Woo, "Religious Ideals, Beliefs and Practices in the Lives of Women during the Reign of T'ang Ming Huang" (PhD diss., University of Toronto, 2000), 144.

B: Woo, Terry Tak-ling. "Religious Ideals, Beliefs and Practices in the Lives of Women during the Reign of T'ang Ming Huang." PhD diss., University of Toronto, 2000.

JOURNAL ARTICLES

N: 19. Brian K. Smith, "Canonical Authority and Social Classification: Veda and Varna in Ancient Indian Texts," *History of Religions* 32 (1992): 119.

B: Smith, Brian K. "Canonical Authority and Social Classification: Veda and Varna in Ancient Indian Texts." *History of Religions* 32 (1992): 103–25.

N: 20. A. E. Harvey, "The Use of Mystery Language in the Bible," *Journal of Theological Studies*, n.s., 31 (1980): 328.

B: Harvey, A. E. "The Use of Mystery Language in the Bible." *Journal of Theological Studies*, n.s., 31 (1980): 320–36.

Note that the bibliography entry gives the inclusive pages of the article.

MAGAZINE ARTICLES
N: 21. Philip Jenkins, "The Next Christianity," *The Atlantic Monthly* 290, no. 3 (October 2002): 59.
B: Jenkins, Philip. "The Next Christianity." *The Atlantic Monthly* 290, no. 3 (October 2002): 53–68.

NEWSPAPER ARTICLES
N: 22. Peter Steinfels, "Amid Islam's Complexity, Scholars Are Challenged to Influence Change without Compromising," Beliefs, *New York Times*, September 29, 2001, D3.
B: Steinfels, Peter. "Amid Islam's Complexity, Scholars Are Challenged to Influence Change without Compromising." Beliefs. *New York Times*, September 29, 2001, D3.

If the article is from a regular column, the name of the column follows the title of the article. If the article is unsigned, the name of the newspaper is moved to the beginning of the citation.

WRITTEN PERSONAL CORRESPONDENCE
N: 23. Shaye J. D. Cohen, e-mail message to author, August 19, 2001.

It is usually unnecessary to provide formal documentation for written personal correspondence (the words 'private communication to author' in parentheses are sufficient), but if you or someone else might want to examine this correspondence someday, it makes sense to document it properly in a note. There is no point adding a bibliography entry for a personal e-mail or an unarchived letter, because it is not something one could find in a library.

SUBSEQUENT REFERENCES TO A BOOK, ARTICLE, OR REVIEW,
USING A SHORTENED TITLE
N: 24. Brown, *Death of the Messiah*, 1:367.
  25. Wolf, "Gods," 136.
  26. McCutcheon, review of *Savage Systems*, 73.
  27. Potter, "Cantonese Shamanism," 215.

QUOTATIONS DERIVED SECOND–HAND
N: 28. Wolfgang Iser, *The Act of Reading: A Theory of Aesthetic Response* (Baltimore and London: Johns Hopkins University Press, 1978), 170, quoted in Robert M. Fowler, *Let the Reader Understand: Reader-Response Criticism and the Gospel of Mark* (Minneapolis: Fortress, 1991), 203.
B: Iser, Wolfgang. *The Act of Reading: A Theory of Aesthetic Response*, 170. Baltimore and London: Johns Hopkins University Press, 1978. Quoted in Robert M. Fowler, *Let the Reader Understand: Reader-Response Criticism and the Gospel of Mark* (Minneapolis: Fortress, 1991), 203.

This format indicates that you have not read the source of your quotation but instead found the quotation in another work. If you subsequently read the source yourself, it is unnecessary to cite the book which led you to the quotation, although if you utilize the quotation in the same way as the other author, you could use this format to acknowledge your intellectual debt. In that case you might modify 'quoted in' like this: 'The relevance of this quotation was noted in . . .' Note that in the bibliography entry, the second-hand source for the quotation is cited in note format rather than bibliography format, because this part of the citation is an annotation to the main bibliography entry; note also the presence and position of the page numbers.

Electronic Secondary Literature
The format for electronic resources is the same as that for printed secondary literature, except that the citation ends

with an internet URL. These entries always end with a period. If the electronic source has page numbers, include them in the citation. The URL is preceded by a comma, except in bibliography entries that include the pagination. In those cases, the URL follows a period yet begins with a lowercase letter. If the provider of the internet resource offers a stable URL (look for a notation describing how to cite this source), cite that URL rather than the one that appeared in your Internet browser's address line, which might be more complicated if you located the resource via a search for particular terms. If you wish to insert a line break in a long URL, avoid placing the break after a period, which might create the appearance of terminal punctuation.

BOOKS, JOURNAL ARTICLES, AND REVIEWS ON THE INTERNET

N: 29. Jeremy R. Carrette, ed., *William James and* The Varieties of Religious Experience: *A Centenary Celebration* (London: Routledge, 2005), http://simplelink.library.utoronto.ca/url.cfm/8936.

B: Carrette, Jeremy R., ed. *William James and* The Varieties of Religious Experience: *A Centenary Celebration*. London: Routledge, 2005, http://simplelink.library.utoronto.ca/url.cfm/8936.

N: 30. William Closson James, review of *Trail to Heaven: Knowledge and Narrative in a Northern Native Community*, by Robin Ridington, *Journal of the American Academy of Religion* 59 (1991): 864–66, http://links.jstor.org/sici?sici=0002-7189%28199124%2959%3A4%3C864%3ATHKAN%3E2.0.CO%3B2-S.

B: James, William Closson. Review of *Trail to Heaven: Knowledge and Narrative in a Northern Native Community*, by Robin Ridington. *Journal of the American Academy of Religion* 59 (1991): 864–66. http://links.jstor.org/sici?sici=0002-7189%28199124%2959%3A4%3C864%3ATHKAN%3E2.0.CO%3B2-S.

INTERNET WEBSITES

N: 31. Bahá'ís International Community, "How Do Bahá'ís Relate to Politics?" The Bahá'ís: International Website of the Bahá'í Faith, http://www.bahai.org/faq/social_action/politics.

B: Bahá'ís International Community. "How Do Bahá'ís Relate to Politics?" The Bahá'ís: International Website of the Bahá'í Faith, http://www.bahai.org/faq/social _action/politics.

If the author is unnamed, list the owner or sponsor of the site as the author. The name of the website follows the title of the article.

INTERNET ENCYCLOPEDIAS

N: 32. Alan Chan, "Laozi," *The Stanford Encyclopedia of Philosophy* (Summer 2007 Edition), ed. Edward N. Zalta, http://plato.stanford.edu/archives/sum2007/entries/laozi/ (accessed May 15, 2007).

B: Chan, Alan. "Laozi." *The Stanford Encyclopedia of Philosophy* (Summer 2007 Edition), edited by Edward N. Zalta, http://plato.stanford.edu/archives/sum2007/entries/laozi/ (accessed May 15, 2007).

N: 33. Oliver Leaman, "Islamic Philosophy," *Routledge Encyclopedia of Philosophy* (1998), ed. Edward Craig (London: Routledge), http://www.rep.routledge.com/article/H057 (accessed May 15, 2007).

B: Leaman, Oliver. "Islamic Philosophy." *Routledge Encyclopedia of Philosophy* (1998), edited by Edward Craig. London: Routledge, http://www.rep.routledge.com/article/H057 (accessed May 15, 2007).

ELECTRONIC MAILING LISTS

N: 34. Robert J. Miller, "[Excavating-Q] Q and the Historical Jesus," e-mail to Synoptic-S mailing list, Nov 9, 2000, http://groups.yahoo.com/group/Synoptic-S/message/34.

B: Miller, Robert J. "[Excavating-Q] Q and the Historical Jesus." E-mail to Synoptic-S mailing list, Nov 9, 2000, http://groups.yahoo.com/group/Synoptic-S/message/34.

Sample Standard Bibliography

Works Cited

Anderson, Leona M., and Pamela Dickey Young. *Women and Religious Traditions*. Don Mills, ON: Oxford University Press, 2004.

Booth, Wayne C. *The Rhetoric of Fiction*. 2nd ed. Chicago: University of Chicago Press, 1983.

Booth, Wayne C., Gregory G. Colomb, and Joseph M. Williams. *The Craft of Research*. 2nd ed. Chicago Guides to Writing, Editing, and Publishing. Chicago: University of Chicago Press, 2003.

Cox, Caroline, and John Marks. *The West, Islam and Islamism: Is Ideological Islam Compatible with Liberal Democracy?* 2nd ed. London: Civitas: The Institute for the Study of Civil Society, 2006.

Creel, Herrlee G. *Chinese Thought from Confucius to Mao Tse-Tung*. 1953. Reprint, Chicago: University of Chicago Press, 1965.

Falk, Daniel K. *Daily, Sabbath, and Festival Prayers in the Dead Sea Scrolls*. Studies on the Texts of the Desert of Judah 27. Leiden and Boston: Brill, 1998.

Hussain, Amir. *Oil and Water: Two Faiths: One God*. Kelowna, BC: CopperHouse, 2006.

King, Winston L. *In the Hope of Nibbana: Theravada Buddhist Ethics*. LaSalle, IL: Open Court, 1964.

Smith, Morton. "Historical Method in the Study of Religion." In *Studies in Historical Method, Ancient Israel, Ancient*

Judaism. Vol. 1 of *Studies in the Cult of Yahweh*, edited by Shaye J. D. Cohen, 3–11. Leiden: Brill, 1996.

————. "The Jewish Elements in the Gospels." *Journal of Bible and Religion* 24 (1956): 90–96.

Sweetman, Will. *Mapping Hinduism: "Hinduism" and the Study of Indian Religions, 1600–1776*. Halle: Franckesche Stiftungen, 2003.

Vaage, Leif E., and Vincent L. Wimbush, eds., *Asceticism and the New Testament*. New York: Routledge, 1999.

Walker, Janice R., and Todd W. Taylor. *The Columbia Guide to Online Style*. 2nd ed. New York: Columbia University Press, 2006.

Yan, Zhonghu. "Self-Cultivation, Society and Metaphysics: An Existential Reading of the 'Analects' (Confucius, China)." PhD diss., University of Toronto, 2004.

British Punctuation of the Standard Format for References

The preceding examples of documentation follow American conventions of punctuation. Authors following British conventions may (if they choose) use single quotation marks around titles that belong inside quotation marks, but they are obliged to place the commas and periods outside the closing quotation mark for these titles. Other differences occur with respect to abbreviations. The American abbreviation **ed.** for 'edition' becomes **edn** in British style, and the abbreviations **pbk.** for 'paperback' and **rpt.** for 'reprint' become **pbk** and **rpt**, likewise losing the period. The periods are dropped from British abbreviations whenever the last letter of the abbreviation is also the last letter of the complete word, since, arguably, these are contractions rather than abbreviations. Thus, **ed.** for 'editor' and **vol.** for 'volume' are abbreviations requiring a period, whereas **eds** for 'editors' and **vols** for 'volumes' are unpunctuated contractions; they are followed by a period only when the punctuation of the bibliography format requires a period. British style likewise uses the 2-em dash in place of the 3-em dash. Consider the following examples:

N: 35. P. J. Bearman et al., eds, *The Encyclopaedia of Islam*, 2nd edn, 17 vols (Leiden: E. J. Brill, 1960–2006).

B: Bearman, P. J., Th. Bianquis, C. E. Bosworth, E. van Donzel and W. P. Heinrichs, eds. *The Encyclopaedia of Islam*. 2nd edn. 17 vols. Leiden: E. J. Brill, 1960–2006.

N: 36. John S. Kloppenborg, 'Isis and Sophia in the Book of Wisdom', *Harvard Theological Review* 75 (1982): 60.

B: ——. 'Isis and Sophia in the Book of Wisdom'. *Harvard Theological Review* 75 (1982): 57–84.

The Author–Date Method

This in-text method is becoming increasingly common in Religious Studies. Rather than using footnotes or endnotes, writers replace the note call-outs with pairs of parentheses containing the relevant pages and just enough information about the work for the reader to locate it in the reference list (i.e. the bibliography). Usually, only three items of information are required: the author's surname,[5] the year of publication, and the page numbers. The format looks like this: (Broadhurst 2002, 804). Occasionally you will see this method used without page numbers in some disciplines within the humanities, but in Religious Studies, unless you are citing the entire work or a work without pagination, you must give the exact pages containing the ideas you present; otherwise, people who want to read those pages for themselves will have to hunt through the entire work.

The following is an example of an in-text reference using the author–date method; imagine that it is an excerpt from a paragraph: 'The specific wording "to his disciples and to Peter" in Mark 16:7 is often viewed as a passing reference to an early resurrection tradition naming Peter as the first to whom Jesus appeared (e.g. Fuller 1971, 57–58, 63–64; Stein

1991, 144). Though such an allusion is plausible . . .' Notice that in this example the parenthetical reference is put immediately *before* the terminal punctuation in its sentence and includes all the relevant pages. If, however, the parenthetical reference comes at the end of a block quotation, it should be put *after* the terminal punctuation (usually a period), with one space separating the period and the opening parenthesis. Consider this example:

> The bulk of totem pole figures . . . symbolizes familiar animals, legends and natural phenomena . . . These symbols were property marks on the houses and household effects and ceremonial carvings of the owners. They were not pagan gods nor demons, as they are often supposed to be. They are comparable to the stylized figures in our heraldry, yet they usually illustrate myths or tribal traditions. (Barbeau 1942, 510)

Some students are confused by the different placement of the parentheses in relation to the period in block quotations and try to harmonize the two conventions, either by stranding the parentheses between sentences in running text or by putting periods before and after the parenthetical references. Bad ideas. I have it on good authority that when Moses descended Mount Sinai carrying the fifteen commandments, the tablet that shattered when he accidentally dropped it contained the words 'Thou shalt not strand thy parentheses nor misuse the period by terminating thy sentences twice.' Certainly scholars argue over what this would have meant in the days before punctuation, but the moral for our time is clear enough.

If you clearly specify the author of a study in the lead up to your in-text reference, it is unnecessary to repeat that person's surname in the parentheses. Instead, begin the reference with the year. In some instances, additional bibliographical information must be added to in-text references. For two or three authors or editors, all surnames are given, whereas for more than three authors or editors, only the first is given, followed by et al.; consider this example: (Duling and Perrin 1994, 60; Mascia-Lees, Sharpe, and Cohen 1989, 7; Holt et al. 1970, 87). When authors in your reference list share the same surname, add these authors' first initials (or as much clarification as necessary) in order to avoid confusion. In order to cite a particular volume in a multi-volume work, add the volume number before the page(s) and separate them with a colon: (de Bary 1960, 2:34).

The reference list at the end of the essay contains the same information that appears in regular bibliographies, and takes the same form as regular bibliographies, with a few differences. The year of the work follows the author, rather than appearing at the end of an entry:

Broadhurst, Laurence. 2002. Review of *Christian–Jewish Relations through the Centuries*, edited by Stanley E. Porter and Brook W. R. Pearson. *Catholic Biblical Quarterly* 64:802–804.

There are other differences between bibliographies and reference lists that *The Chicago Manual of Style* considers optional; students wishing to further complicate their lives may consult Chicago.

Sample Author–Date Bibliography

When writers cite many works by the same author, they sometimes prefer a variant in the formatting of reference lists that displays the year of publication more prominently. I use this variant in the following sample bibliography:

Works cited

Barbeau, Marius.

    1942   "Totem Poles: A By-product of the Fur Trade." *The Scientific Monthly* 55, no. 6:507–14.

Duling, Dennis C., and Norman Perrin.

    1994   *The New Testament: An Introduction. Proclamation*

and Parenesis, Myth and History. 3rd ed. Fort Worth: Harcourt Brace.

Eliade, Mircea.

1954   *The Myth of the Eternal Return: Cosmos and History*. Translated by Willard R. Trask. Bollingen Series 46. New York: Pantheon Books. Reprinted with a new introduction by Jonathan Z. Smith. 2nd pbk. ed. Princeton: Princeton University Press, 2005.

1959   *The Sacred and the Profane: The Nature of Religion*. Translated by Willard R. Trask. London: Harcourt Brace Jovanovich.

1963   "The History of Religions in Retrospect: 1912–1962." *Journal of Bible and Religion* 31:98–109.

Holt, Peter Malcolm, Ann K. S. Lambton, and Bernard Lewis, eds.

1970   *The Cambridge History of Islam*. 2 vols. Cambridge: Cambridge University Press.

Marsden, George M.

1992   "The Soul of the American University: An Historical Overview." In *The Secularization of the Academy*, edited with Bradley J. Longfield, 9–45. New York: Oxford University Press.

1997a   "Christian Advocacy and the Rules of the Academic Game." In *Religious Advocacy and American History*, edited by Bruce Kuklick and D. G. Hart, 3–27. Grand Rapids: Eerdmans.

1997b   *The Outrageous Idea of Christian Scholarship*. New York: Oxford University Press.

Mascia-Lees, Francis E., Patricia Sharpe, and Colleen Ballerino Cohen.

    1989   "The Postmodern Turn in Anthropology: Cautions from a Feminist Perspective." *Signs* 15:7–33.

Although the order of authors in reference lists is alphabetical, the order of works by individual authors is the order of publication, except when multiple works by an author are listed for the same year, in which case those particular items are arranged alphabetically by title and are distinguished with letters. Those letters also appear in the parenthetical references: (Marsden 1997b, 32).

Gender-Inclusive Language

Most publishers and readers today appreciate it when authors use gender-inclusive language. The words *man* and *he* have primarily masculine connotations today, and therefore are problematic when used as gender-neutral terms. Notice, for example, how words constructed with *man* can convey the impression that humanity is a collective of males (e.g. mankind, layman, the average man, the man in the street, man-made) or that the workplace is the domain of men (e.g. alderman, chairman, foreman, spokesman, middleman, repairman). In most cases, there are inclusive (or gender-neutral) substitutes: humankind, persons, humans, humanity, layperson, most people, synthetic, councillor, chairperson, chair, foreperson, spokesperson, go-between, intermediary, facilitator, technician. Unfortunately, the word *he* (as a neuter pronoun) is much harder to replace. The usual solutions are to substitute phrases (e.g. he or she, that person, that individual, that one) or to reuse the noun itself. But when these phrases are used repeatedly, they become cumbersome and tedious. So you may need to be creative. Sometimes a sentence can be rewritten in a way that removes the need for the pronoun. Occasionally, the subject of the sentence can be changed to a plural so that the corresponding pronoun is plural. At present, the use of *they* as a replacement for *he* still looks to many people like a grammatical error of subject–pronoun agreement, and this solution is rarely adopted in published formal writing. Some writers use *she* as a replacement for *he* as a neuter personal pronoun, or alternate using *she* and *he*. This solution does not really solve the problem, though, which is the use of gendered language when a gender is not implied. Other writers use *he/she* and *him/her* – constructions that can sound a bit abrupt. Writing *s/he* or *(s)he* can be slightly confusing to the reader, who may need to pause to figure out what a s/he is (there is also no parallel construction for the object form, 'her and him'). The lack of a neuter third-person singular personal pronoun will probably remain an annoyance until someone invents one that catches on.

A related matter is gender balance. Some advocates of gender equality in writing have pointed out that the gender order of common phrases such as 'men and women', 'male and female', 'boys and girls', 'he or she', 'husband and wife', and 'Mr and Mrs' perpetuates a masculine bias. These writers suggest varying the gender order of such phrases or substituting terms that do not refer to gender (e.g. sometimes writing 'people' or 'women and men' in place of 'men and women').

Using gender-inclusive language is as much a matter of precision and clarity as it is of being sensitive to how others might construe the implications of our words. In academic writing, whenever our words could be understood as conveying meanings we do not intend, we need to find more precise ways of stating things. Moreover, as a matter of principle, we need to recognize and confront the biases that are built into our language systems, because these biases shape the way we think about things. We are less likely to discover new ways of looking at issues if we remain unaware of the preconceptions that lead us to see issues in the usual ways.

Layout

Your essay should have a title page containing the title, your name, the course number, the name of the instructor, the date due, and the date *submitted* (if the paper is late). Titles on title pages should not be put in quotation marks or italicized (all caps are unnecessary, but acceptable); and they do not end with a period. (A title placed in the centre of the page in bold type can be effective.) You do not need to repeat any of this information at the top of page 1. Although many students like to put their work in attractive binders (with cute butterfly stickers), these can be cumbersome for the grader: a staple in the top left corner is sufficient (if you use endnotes or the author–date method you might want to use a secure clip rather than a staple so that the grader can remove the documentation for easier reference). Laser printers are preferable for printing text.

The body of the essay should be double spaced, with margins that are at least 3 to 3.5 cm (about 1.25 inches) on both sides and at the top, and 2.5 to 3 cm (1 inch) at the bottom. This should give your grader enough room to put comments in the margins and between the lines of text. Margins any larger than 4 cm (1.5 inches) might give your grader the impression that you are trying to make a short essay look longer (graders know all the tricks – they were once undergraduates, too). The body of the essay should be in a standard 12-point font such as Times New Roman, along with the endnotes (if you use them) and the bibliography; footnotes and block quotations should be one font size smaller.

The pages of your essay must be numbered; this will allow your grader to refer to specific pages when writing a separate page of comments. Treat the title page as page 0 and suppress the numbering for that page (some style manuals recommend suppressing the numbering for page 1 as well, so that the numerals first begin to show on page 2).

Make sure that headings are distinguished in some visual way from ordinary text (e.g. by being in bold font) and that each level of heading is visually distinct from the other levels. The upper levels should be the most prominent. You can make an upper-level heading more prominent by centring it and using a larger font size (e.g. 16-point) and more space before and after it. Your word processor is probably already set up to apply a set of attributes to any line of text formatted as a particular heading level.

Safeguarding Your Work

Back when I was a graduate student, computer hard-drive space was at a premium, and strange contraptions called floppy disks were used to store copies of files or to transport them between computers. I had little room for superfluous files, so I kept each of my essays in one file, relying on my word processor to make a backup copy each time I opened a file. Then one day my computer lost power while I was working on a term paper, and when I rebooted the computer and reopened the file, nothing was there. My word processor had automatically made a backup of this empty file, leaving me with nothing. I lost two months of work through a simple series of misfortunes. So I started keeping several backup files on different disks, and updated one of those copies after every work session. I also periodically copied those files onto my relatives' computers so that they would not all be under one roof. Those precautions prevented more misfortune.

Today, we have plenty of hard-drive space and high-capacity storage devices, so in place of writing over backup copies, I recommend saving a complete series of earlier versions of your essays under different file names (e.g. RLG241Y_Essay_12.doc) and keeping copies of all these files on external storage devices. I save my essays under modified file numbers every day or two, as well as every time I make a significant revision that might not be an improvement. That way, if I lose the file I am working on, I never lose more than one or two days' work, and when my latest experiment in revising is a failure, I can go back to the file I saved immediately before it. Should I want to add something that I excised from my essay weeks ago, I still have several earlier versions in which to find it. Retaining a complete series of earlier versions of a paper has an added advantage for students. It provides them with evidence that they wrote the paper themselves.

It is a very bad idea to delete your essay files once you have submitted the essay. As conscientious as your graders try to be, they are subject to the same 'acts of God' that plague you. If the grader's pet Chihuahua eats your essay, you will be the only person who can produce another copy. If you use a typewriter or any other primitive writing device, such as quill and ink, make a photocopy of your essay to keep for yourself (submit the original, not the copy). Better yet, get a computer!

Notes

[1] In a highly influential book, Edward W. Said argued that Western academics have often characterized 'the Oriental' as innately backward, irrational, and malleable, in a way that helped justify Western domination. See his *Orientalism*, 25th Anniversary edn, with a new preface by the author (New York: Pantheon Books, 1978; New York: Vintage Books, 2003).

[2] Occasionally, one encounters a journal or book series in which the members of the editorial review committee are also the main contributors. These 'publication clubs' allow mediocre scholars to avoid the strictures of peer review by approving each other's work.

[3] James R. Kennedy, Jr, *Library Research Guide to Religion and Theology: Illustrated Search Strategy and Sources*, 2nd rev. edn, Library Research Guides Series 1 (Ann Arbor: Pierian, 1984), 21.

[4] Gordon D. Fee, *New Testament Exegesis: A Handbook for Students and Pastors*, 3rd edn (Louisville: Westminster John Knox, 2002), 34. The preceding recommendations of when to quote are based on Fee's discussion.

[5] I refer to the author's surname for convenience. There could be one or more authors, editors, or translators, or a committee or corporation.

2 Approaching Ancient Texts

The authors of ancient texts inhabited worlds that were very different from our own. The cultural and historical gap between us and them makes these texts especially challenging to understand. John H. Hayes and Carl R. Holladay illustrate this problem using the example of an old newspaper. If you were to read a newspaper from fifty years ago, you would have some difficulty making sense of the issues that were important then, the predominant attitudes, the style of reporting.[1] You might not recognize persons whose names required no explanation. In other words, you would need to study the history, culture, and ethos of that time and place in order to understand the newspaper in a way that approximates what it meant to the original readers. Now imagine a text from hundreds or thousands of years ago and from another part of the world. The gap is considerably greater. The differences between our ways of thinking and those of the original audience might not appear to be so great to someone for whom an ancient text is scripture. People generally assume that their religion has preserved the values, ideas, and background information necessary to make these texts readily comprehensible to people within that tradition. But if you study a religion long enough, you realize that the immediacy of the communication is mostly illusory. The world is always changing, so the values and ideas presupposed by the author have constantly been reinterpreted and translated into more contemporary ways of thinking, and much of the background information has been forgotten. In a book written for evangelical Christians, D. A. Carson gives this apt example: 'We hear the Word of God commanding us to take up our cross and follow the Lord Jesus Christ, and so read our experience into the text that our "cross" becomes rheumatism, shortage of money, an irascible relative, an awkward roommate, [or] a personal defect.' To someone who lived in Jesus' society, however, where taking up a cross meant being 'condemned to die the painful, ignominious, humiliating death Rome reserved for noncitizen criminals, the scum of the earth',[2] this was a call to follow a politically subversive way of life that might result in execution as an enemy of the state. It is impossible to appreciate what these words communicated in Jesus' day without learning about his society.

The first precept of Buddhism supplies another example. Western Buddhists often interpret the precept 'to abstain from killing' as prescribing vegetarianism. Certainly vegetarianism is wholly compatible with this precept. Yet the precept itself does not refer to diet, and the first Buddhists did not interpret it as limiting what they could eat. Rather, Buddhist monks and nuns aspired to non-attachment and equanimity with respect to their food, eating whatever they were offered. Their diet was limited only insofar as they would not kill animals for food or ask others to do so. When Western Buddhists interpret the intention behind this precept in terms of vegetarianism, they are reading a different value system into the precept.

In order to bridge the cultural and historical gap between us and a religious text, we need to learn about the historical context in which it was written: the social, intellectual, and cultural milieus of the author. We also need to study other texts that disclose the author's life and thought, and to learn whatever we can about the text's intended readers, specific occasion, literary genre (and subgenres), and composition history.

The Author

By mentioning the author, I am again raising a sensitive issue for some students. Few would deny that the vast majority of religious writings were authored in the same way as other texts. However, many religions downplay or completely deny any human factor in the creation of their most important writings, their scriptures, as a way of affirming the distinctive reliability and authority of these particular texts. Thus tradition maintains that the Vedas have no authors but consist of eternal knowledge that seers heard. The Buddhist Tipitaka consists of discourses of the enlightened Buddha that were remembered verbatim by monks with phenomenal memories, then fixed in early councils and faithfully transmitted from teacher to student by rote memorization until they were written down. The Ten Commandments were inscribed by the finger of God, and the Torah was dictated to Moses by God himself. The four gospel writers faithfully transmitted what they remembered (or heard from eye-witnesses) under the guidance of the Holy Spirit. Muhammad was illiterate and received the Qur'an as a series of revelations from God delivered by an angel; the Qur'an is literarily superior to any human work and inimitable. This idea of a perfect book untainted by human authorship is so common among religions that some people consider it axiomatic that Ultimate Truth is a writer and therefore that 'the One True Religion' is the one whose scripture contains the most supernaturally inspired content. Yet as attractive as this idea of the perfect book has been, even the most conservative scholars of religion who work in (Western) public universities cannot deny that the contents of their own scriptures make far more sense when the human factor is not minimized or denied. Hence in their capacity as historians they conceive of scriptures as mediums through which particular people or groups attempted to influence the attitudes and behaviours of others around them. The only way you can decide for yourself whether this historical-critical approach is valid is by trying it and discovering whether it helps you better understand these texts.

Accepting that a text contains the thoughts of its human author is but the first step. We also want to know, if possible, who this person was. Our understanding of a religious text is always enhanced when we can situate it in relation to other works by the same individual and within a particular period of the author's life. Accordingly, scholars consult other writings by that author and *reliable* second-hand sources, if any exist. Unfortunately, the authors sometimes prove elusive. In some cases, the author chose to remain anonymous. In other cases, an anonymous text has been piously mis-attributed to a famous individual (e.g. the legendary Lao Tzu as the author of the Tao Te Ching), or an obscure writer deliberately impersonated a famous person in order to reach a wider audience (e.g. at least three and possibly as many as six of the thirteen letters attributed to the apostle Paul are by persons pretending to be him). It is hard to overstate the prevalence of anonymity and false attribution among religious texts.

The Intended Readers

A different set of problems surround the intended audiences of religious texts. Because many religions develop a universal orientation, people sometimes suppose that the authors of religious texts envisioned the widest audiences possible, but that was rarely the case. The audiences are normally quite specific. Many Buddhist texts, for instance, begin with the words 'O monks'. Those texts do not concern lay Buddhists, even though lay Western Buddhists sometimes suppose that any Buddhist is in view. The implied audience for the Vedas likewise varies. For example, the mantras contained in the Atharva Veda were probably intended for the priestly class, whereas the hymns of the Rig Veda might have been directed to a more general audience. Some Taoist and Confucian texts are clearly directed at persons in government

and attempt to convert rulers to their vision of how to run
the affairs of state. The Torah is specifically for the people of
Israel, and is mostly concerned with the men, even though
Christians usually imagine themselves as part of the intended
audience. Most of the undisputed letters of the apostle Paul
were written to his own converts in particular cities or
regions (e.g. Rome, Corinth, Galatia) and address issues
within those communities.

Although the authors of religious texts were usually
writing for a specific audience, they did not always clearly
indicate who they had in view. Nevertheless, we can learn a
fair bit about these people by noting how the author envisioned them. Every writer addresses either a specific group of
people or a specific kind of person, and makes assumptions
about what these people know and do not know. I am doing
that myself. I do not know my readers personally, but I have
a definite conception of what kind of people they are
(undergraduate university students taking a religion course)
that helps me decide what I need to spell out for them and
what I can presuppose they already know. The authors of
religious texts did the same thing. Regardless of whether
they knew their readers personally, they had a mental conception of these readers. We can develop a profile of these
implied readers by going through a text sentence by sentence
and noting everything that the author presupposes that the
readers already know or do not know. (A study like this
could form the basis for a highly original essay.) Sometimes
small details betray a great deal. The author of the Gospel of
Mark, for instance, assumes that his readers do not know the
language of the Jewish characters in the story (e.g. 5:41) or
the value of the type of coin that a widow put in the temple
treasury (12:42). He thereby tells us that he is not imagining
his readers as native inhabitants of Palestine. On the other
hand, he supposes that his readers know and accept the
authority of the Jewish scriptures, and he introduces certain
characters, such as Pilate (the Roman governor of Judea at
the time of Jesus), without explaining who they are. By

examining all these clues, one can deduce that Mark's audience consisted of Christians who spoke Greek but not Aramaic and therefore lived somewhere outside of Palestine and Syria.[3] This is important information.

The Reason or Occasion for Writing

Generally speaking, the religious texts that historians learn the most from are the ones written by known individuals to known recipients in known circumstances. In ideal cases, the principal historical figures and situations are adequately described in the texts themselves. For instance, there is enough contextual information in the Qur'an for historians to situate its suras (chapters) within the broad outline of Muhammad's career and to examine their messages in relation to the socio-political conditions that they explicitly addressed. This approach highlights the reciprocal relationship between the first community of believers and Muhammad's revelations, shedding much light on the earliest period of Islam. In other cases there is no particular occasion for a text, but the author nevertheless had a purpose. The author of the Gospel of John, for instance, explained his purpose explicitly: 'these [things] are written that you may [continue to] believe that Jesus is the Christ, the Son of God, and that believing you may have life in his name' (20:31; Revised Standard Version). More often than not, however, all knowledge of the authors, original audiences, and purposes or occasioning situations has been lost to time. Although in these cases we can still understand *what* the author was saying, we do not know why, so we cannot assess the text's original significance – only its significance to later generations. For that reason, whenever we do not know for certain the author, the intended readers, or the reason for writing or circumstance being addressed, we develop hypotheses about these things, relying on analogous elements in other documents from roughly the same period. The process is inherently speculative, but by developing hypotheses and evaluating their ability to explain a text's contents, the most diligent scholars improve our understanding of that text and sometimes do squeeze blood from a stone.

The Genre

Although one can understand the basic meaning of a text without understanding why it was relevant to its first hearers, one cannot understand even its basic meaning without knowing the kind of text it represents – its genre. Is the book a letter, a treatise, a sermon, an apocalypse, a sutra, a prophetic work, a biography, a novel? Does it contain subgenres such as maxims, proverbs, legal pronouncements, chreiai, parables, fables, oracles, spells, poems, myths? All of these forms of communication have their own conventions, and if you misunderstand these conventions, you will misunderstand what the author intended to convey. Someone unfamiliar with modern conventions of letter-writing might, for instance, mistakenly presume that the greeting 'Dear so-and-so' implies strong feelings of affection for the addressee, only to discover after reading many examples of modern letters that the word *dear* is purely conventional and sometimes ironic, as when the correspondents dislike each other so much that they refuse to talk face-to-face. Likewise, a modern reader of an ancient apocalypse needs to know the conventions of apocalyptic writing. Many people mistakenly suppose that the visions in these writings describe modern situations and technologies using the only words and images that the author had available to describe such things. In reality, these works are always concerned with the immediate future of their original recipients, and describe this future in hyperbolically symbolic images that were not supposed to be taken literally. For example, the seer of the quintessential apocalypse, Revelation, described the destruction of Rome – figuratively called Babylon – in several ways: In 16:17–21 Rome is destroyed by a colossal earthquake. The imagery in 17:16 suggests that Rome will be sacked and burned by an army led by a former emperor. In 18:2 Rome's fate is described in terms of it becoming the haunt of desert creatures. But in 19:3 it is described as burning eternally with smoke ascending forever. These images of the fate of Rome do not fit together logically. Nor were they supposed to. They are alternative ways of portraying the idea of Rome's judgement and destruction.

The Stages of Composition

Finally, you need to know about the evolution of an ancient text. Not all religious texts were written by one individual. Frequently, the principal author utilized other authors' writings as raw materials for a new work, not always acknowledging his use of sources. Less frequently, subsequent authors deliberately revised the text, usually by adding sentences or whole sections. Scholars have developed criteria for isolating these sources and later additions, although their reconstructions of a work's composition history are often speculative. In some cases, however, we can be quite certain that a particular passage was not written by the principal author because it differs in style or outlook and, more importantly, does not appear in the oldest and best manuscripts. We are certain, for instance, that the story of the woman caught in adultery in the Gospel of John 7:53–8:11 is a later addition and that the last twelve verses of the Gospel of Mark (16:9–20) were added several decades later. Chapters 40–55 of the Jewish scripture Isaiah not only differ in style from the first part of this writing but also reflect an historical setting that existed long after the time of the prophet Isaiah, and chapters 56–66 reflect yet another period in Israel's history. When analysing a text, you need to know which passages were not likely written by the principal author so that you do not confuse a subsequent author's opinions for those of the person who wrote the main book.

You can find this information in scholarly commentaries on that text.

Notes

[1] John H. Hayes and Carl R. Holladay, *Biblical Exegesis: A Beginner's Handbook* (Atlanta: John Knox, 1982), 10.

[2] D. A. Carson, *Exegetical Fallacies* (Grand Rapids: Baker Book House, 1984), 105–106.

[3] See Ernest Best, 'Mark's Readers: A Profile', in *The Four Gospels 1992: Festschrift Frans Neirynck*, ed. Frans Van Segbroeck et al., Bibliotheca Ephemeridum Theologicarum Lovaniensium 100 (Leuven: Leuven University Press, 1992), 2:839–58.

3 Some Finer Points of Writing, for More Experienced Students

Style

Many students have never been taught the rules of grammar and punctuation, not to mention the technical aspects of style, such as which words to capitalize in a title. This sort of information may be found in style manuals and writer's handbooks, such as the ones listed in the appendix. Brief but very useful discussions of style often appear at the back of large dictionaries, along with examples of documentation methods, lists of standard abbreviations, guidelines for punctuation, and other information relevant to formal writing. Many universities have their own websites devoted to grammar and style, which are readily found with a search engine. These explain the most common grammatical errors, such as sentence fragment, faulty parallelism, anacoluthon, dangling participle, misplaced modifier, run-on sentence, and comma splice. If you do not know what these terms mean, you probably make these mistakes now and then. I cannot stress too strongly the importance of a style manual for a university student, because people have no idea that they make mistakes in their writing until they learn the rules.

British and American Style and Punctuation
The most obvious difference between British and American style concerns the use of quotation marks. British style uses

pairs of single quotation marks around quotations, whereas American style uses pairs of double quotation marks. The British convention becomes a little confusing when a quotation includes a possessive plural, for the apostrophe at the end of these words is the same character as a closing single quotation mark and might look like the end of a quotation. British style is more logical than American style where it comes to commas and periods at the ends of quotations. For aesthetic reasons, American practice puts periods and commas inside (to the left of) closing quotation marks, even when the quoted material does not include a comma or period at that point. British practice puts the period or comma outside (to the right of) the closing quotation mark unless it is part of the original quotation.[1] The two styles agree on the position of question marks, exclamation marks, semicolons, colons, and dashes: those punctuation marks are always outside of the closing punctuation marks, except when question marks and exclamation marks are part of the quotation (semicolons and colons are invariably placed outside).

Another difference between British and American practice concerns the serial comma, which is the last comma in a series of three or more items that are separated by commas. When the last two items in such a series are separated by the word *and* or *or*, American practice places a comma before the conjunction, whereas British practice usually omits it. The British explanation is that the conjunction has the same purpose as the comma, so the comma is redundant. The American response is that without the comma, the relationship between the items in a series is sometimes unclear. Here is a classic example, adapted from an actual book dedication: 'I'd like to thank my parents, Ayn Rand and God.' Is the author thanking three humans here or just one, his mother, who is not only a famous (atheist) author but also the handmaiden of God? In cases such as this, followers of the British convention will make an exception and use a comma before the final *and* or else rewrite the sentence so as to remove the ambiguity: 'I'd like to thank Ayn Rand, my parents and God.'[2] However, as others have pointed out, the serial comma can create confusion, too. What if the author wrote, 'I'd like to thank my mother, Ayn Rand, and God'? Here, the presence of a comma before the *and* makes it unclear whether the author is thanking his mother in addition to Ayn Rand and God or whether the commas around Ayn Rand signify an appositive naming Rand as the author's mother. If the author intends to distinguish between his mother and Ayn Rand, he would do better to revise the order of items or omit the serial comma: 'I'd like to thank my mother, Ayn Rand and God.' The important thing, then, is to be conscious of which convention you use and to use it consistently *except* where it creates ambiguity.

For the differences between American and British punctuation of abbreviations, see 'British Punctuation of the Standard Format for References'.

Punctuation Marks

My remarks on this extensive subject are limited to a few matters of common confusion.

Semicolons and colons

When used at the end of an independent clause, both of these marks indicate that the thought of that clause is not yet complete: something else is coming that is important to the point. The colon (:) does this by way of clarification, amplification, or completion, which is why it normally introduces examples and lists. Sometimes the colon has the same function as the linking adverbs *namely* and *that is*. The semicolon (;), by contrast, gives little guidance about what the connection might be between the clauses; it just signals a close connection in thought. Consider this example from the Gospel of Matthew, in which the voice of God refers to Jesus: 'This is my beloved Son; in him I take great delight' (3:17).[3] This semicolon indicates that the second clause continues the theme of paternal pride, which would be less apparent if the translator used a full stop: 'This is my beloved Son. In him I take great delight.' In unrefined writing, the close connection between two clauses sometimes results from the failure to make the point adequately the first time: 'Jesus spoke all these things in parables to the crowds; he did not speak to them without a parable' (13:34). By contrast, in very refined writing, the connection in thought sometimes involves parallel structure: 'Ask and it will be given to you; seek and you will find; knock and the door will be opened to you' (7:7). 'We played the flute for you, yet you did not dance; we wailed in mourning, yet you did not weep' (11:17).

Semicolons are also used within clauses to clarify divisions within a list. Notice how the use of commas alone both to link items and to add extra information about some items makes this list difficult to comprehend:

> Now these are the names of the twelve apostles: First, Simon (called Peter), and Andrew his brother, James son of Zebedee and John his brother, Philip and Bartholomew, Thomas and Matthew the tax collector, James, the son of Alphaeus, and Thaddaeus, Simon the Zealot and Judas Iscariot, who betrayed him. (Mt. 10:2–4)

The author's pairing of disciples and his additions of explanatory information are much clearer when semicolons mark out the larger divisions:

> Now these are the names of the twelve apostles: First, Simon (called Peter), and Andrew his brother; James son of Zebedee and John his brother; Philip and Bartholomew; Thomas and Matthew the tax collector; James, the son of Alphaeus, and Thaddaeus; Simon the Zealot and Judas Iscariot, who betrayed him.

Exclamation marks
It is odd to find exclamation marks in the midst of impartial analysis. So in formal writing, use this mark when describing

something truly astonishing or exciting – when you might appear unnaturally dispassionate for omitting it – rather than to make something sound more exciting than it is (leave that use to advertisers). Liberal use of exclamation marks can make writing appear disingenuous and emotionally manipulative.

Dashes

When used to connect two related clauses, dashes announce an abrupt change in thought or tone: 'As the poet said, "Only God can make a tree" – probably because it's so hard to figure out how to get the bark on' (Woody Allen). They are also commonly used in place of a pair of commas or parentheses to set off a comment that interrupts a clause: 'The threefold fruit of works – desirable, undesirable, and mixed – accrues after death to one who is not a Tyaagi (Renunciant), but never to a Tyaagi' (Bhagavad-Gita 18:12).[4] Dashes (or parentheses) are preferable for this purpose when the interruption is abrupt or contains its own punctuation (especially when the interruption ends with a question mark or an exclamation mark).

When a sentence begins with a subject that is so elaborate that it must be summarized (usually with a pronoun) in the main clause, the main clause is introduced with a dash:

> The Master said, 'Yu, shall I teach you what knowledge is? When you know a thing, to hold that you know it; and when you do not know a thing, to allow that you do not know it – this is knowledge.' (Confucius, Analects 2:17)

> The Master said, 'Ardent and yet not upright; stupid and yet not attentive; simple and yet not sincere – such persons I do not understand.' (8:16)

> Filial piety and fraternal submission – are they not the root of all benevolent actions? (1:2)[5]

Hyphens and dashes

Dashes are not the same as hyphens. Hyphens (-) are used within or between words (e.g. pre-Vedic, seventh-century Arabia) and are half the width of an en–dash (–), the character used to separate inclusive numerals (for example, 55–60; 1966–70). The other, more familiar form of dash separates phrases and clauses. Adherents of the American convention form this dash using either the em-dash character (—), which is twice the width of an en-dash, or two hyphens (--); no spaces at all come between these forms of the dash and the adjoining words. Adherents of the British convention form this dash using a single en-dash surrounded by single spaces (–), although a closed-up em-dash is also acceptable. Be consistent in the way you form dashes.

Punctuation marks and spaces

There is never a space between square and round brackets and the words within them (note this one). No space precedes punctuation marks (i.e. commas, semicolons, colons, periods, question marks and exclamation marks), though one space comes after them. The same applies to the superscript numbers of note call-outs. An exception occurs with colons when they are used in documentation to separate a chapter from a verse (e.g. Mark 14:51) or a volume in a multi-volume work from the page number.

Quotation marks and italics

A word used in a sense other than its normal one or that needs to be qualified in order to be appropriate is put in quotation marks rather than italics (as in, keep your military 'music' to yourself). American style uses double quotation marks for this purpose; British style usually uses single quotation marks, though double quotation marks are also acceptable. Italics are used instead to emphasize a word or phrase (*do not* use underlining or bold font for this purpose) or to refer to a word as a word (e.g. have you ever considered that the word *abbreviation* is a surprisingly long word?). However, if you are referring to a word as a word in a context in which you are discussing particular words and phrases in a text, it makes sense to use quotation marks instead of italics in order to avoid the inconsistency of using italics for individual words but quotation marks for phrases (e.g. some scholars insist that the word 'mystery' in the expression 'the mystery of the kingdom of God' has no connection to the mystery religions). I indicated earlier that the titles of books are also put in italics when you cite them. This is *not* generally true of religious scriptures, however. Pay attention to which titles of religious texts are italicized in scholarly literature. Finally, italicize individual foreign terms that have not yet been adopted into the English language (check a dictionary if you are unsure) and foreign terms that you have transliterated (meaning rendered in Latin characters).

Introductory Punctuation for Quotations

The punctuation preceding a block quotation is determined by the syntax of the words introducing it. When the introductory words form a complete sentence, use a colon or a period. A colon conveys anticipation for the contents of the quotation. It is the appropriate punctuation mark when the block quotation clarifies or substantiates the introductory sentence, and it is always used when the introductory sentence ends with 'thus' or 'the following'. A period, on the other hand, does not convey anticipation for the quotation and is therefore more appropriate when the block quotation merely continues the thought expressed in the introductory statement rather than clarifying or substantiating it. When the introductory words do not form a complete sentence but do form a complete subordinate phrase whose purpose is to identify the author (such as 'According to Mary Baker Eddy' or 'As Maimonides noted'), use a comma. In these cases, as well as in cases where the introductory words form a complete clause, the first word of the block quotation should be capitalized, regardless of whether it was capitalized in the source (there is no need to use brackets to indicate a change in case). Finally, when the introductory words form an incomplete phrase that is completed syntactically by the opening words of the quotation (e.g. 'C. S. Lewis noted that'), use no punctuation. In these cases, the first word of the block quotation should be lower case unless it is a word that must be capitalized, such as a proper noun (again, brackets denoting a change in case are unnecessary).

Similar considerations apply to run-in quotations, as the following examples illustrate:

> 'Character is doing what's right when nobody's looking', says J. C. Watts.

> 'Character', asserts J. C. Watts, 'is doing what's right when nobody's looking.'

> 'Doing what's right when nobody's looking' – that is how J. C. Watts defines 'character'.

> According to J. C. Watts, 'Character is doing what's right when nobody's looking.'

> J. C. Watts believes that 'character is doing what's right when nobody's looking'.

> J. C. Watts defines 'character' as 'doing what's right when nobody's looking'.

Whether or not the first word of the run-in quotation is capitalized depends on its place in the sentence. In the first three examples, the first word of the quotation is capitalized, regardless of whether it was capitalized in the original statement, because it is now the first word of the sentence. In the fourth example, where the quotation forms a complete clause and the words introducing it form a subordinate clause identifying the author, the first word of the quotation is again capitalized, even if it was lower case in the original. In the final two examples, on the other hand, where the quotation is embedded as part of the main clause, the first word is lower cased.

Ellipsis points

When incorporating a quotation into your essay, you might want to omit inessential words, phrases, and sentences for the sake of brevity or to make the quotation fit the syntax of your paragraph. Indicate these omissions using three dots (no more, no less), called ellipsis points. The three dots are always separated from each other by spaces (. . .) and also from the words of the quotation by one space on either side, as in this repetitious example: 'The three dots are always separated from each other . . . and also from . . . the quotation by one space on either side.' Notice that I did not use ellipsis points at the end of my quotation, even though I omitted the words 'as in this repetitious example'. Quotations are almost always extracts from a larger context, so it is unnecessary to indicate that you omitted the words and sentences that precede and follow them in the original. You may make an exception to alert your reader to the fact that the omitted beginning or end of the sentence contains something that is conceivably relevant to a correct understanding of the quotation. However, ellipsis points should never be used to skew the meaning of a quotation or to eliminate words that conflict with your use of the quotation.

The Chicago Manual of Style describes three different sets of conventions regarding the use of ellipsis points. In the simplest method, which should be sufficient for undergraduate essays, a period never precedes or follows the three ellipsis points, although other essential punctuation marks are retained. Whether or not the first word following the ellipsis points is capitalized depends upon the syntax. 'The first word . . . is capitalized if it begins a grammatically complete sentence, even if it was lowercased in the original' (it is not necessary to put brackets around the changed letter).[6] Add your ellipsis points in such a way that the remaining words form proper sentences.

A line break should not occur within ellipsis points. One way to prevent your word processor from breaking a line within ellipsis points is by separating the three dots with two non-breaking spaces. Another way is by using a special character for ellipsis points that is provided in some programmes. This special character decreases the spacing between the dots by half, significantly reducing the width of the ellipsis points. If you choose to use this character, use it consistently.

Capitalization for Headings and Titles of Works

The same rules of capitalization apply to the titles of works (books, articles, poems, plays, movies, etc.) and to headings and subheadings within works: The first and last words of a title and a subtitle are *always* capitalized (even if they are minor words), along with all major words (nouns, verbs, pronouns, adjectives and adverbs). The remaining minor words (articles, conjunctions, prepositions) are lower case. The first element in a hyphenated word is always capitalized; the second element is lower cased unless it is an adjective or a proper noun. Except when used as the first or last word of the title or subtitle, the preposition *to* is lower cased, even when it is part of an infinitive, and the word *as* is also lower cased, even when it is used as an adverb or a pronoun.

Numbers and Numerals

Numerals are the symbols that represent numbers (0, 1, 2, 3, 4, etc. are Arabic numerals; I, II, III, IV, etc. are Roman numerals). Style manuals tell us never to begin a sentence with a numeral. Thus if you wish to begin a sentence with a numeral, you must either spell it out as a word or rewrite the sentence so that the numeral is not the first element:

> *Wrong*: 1 Corinthians was not the first letter Paul wrote to the church in Corinth.
> *Right*: Paul's first letter to the church in Corinth was not 1 Corinthians.
> *Right*: First Corinthians was not Paul's first letter to the church in Corinth.

In addition to this convention, the practice in the humanities is to spell out all numbers between zero and one hundred, and to use numerals for numbers greater than one hundred, except when these large numbers can be written out as two words (e.g. two hundred, one thousand; twenty-two million; sixty-four billion). Fractions are written out if they can be expressed in one or two words (e.g. half, two-thirds, five-eighths) or, if you prefer, set as numerals if they are longer (e.g. nine and seven-eighths or $9\frac{7}{8}$). The exceptions, which are always set as numerals unless they occur first in a sentence, are years and the other numbers in dates (e.g. Nisan 14, 30 CE; May 29, 2007), page numbers, chapter numbers, and percentages. Of course, if you get into a technical discussion involving precise scientific measurements, you should use numerals (e.g. 8.3 cm; 72 m; 15.7 km).

Unlike years, the numbers of centuries are written out. Whether a hyphen appears between the number and the word *century* depends on whether the number is an adjective modifying the word *century* or whether both the number and the word *century* together modify another word. In the latter case, a hyphen is used to indicate that the two words work together to express one thought:

Wrong: the 5th century; eighteenth century scholarship
Right: the fifth century; eighteenth-century scholarship

Because the fact seems counterintuitive, even historians must remind themselves that the number of the century is one more than the fixed number in the years of that century. Thus the years 399–300 BCE were the fourth century BCE, the years 100–199 CE were the second century CE, and the years 1700–1799 were the eighteenth century.

Inclusive numerals are separated with a special character called an en-dash (a dash the width of the letter *N*) rather than a hyphen. When placed between numerals, this dash is the equivalent of the words *to* or *through*. You would not, however, use an en-dash in place of *to* when you write 'from [this year] to [this year]' or in place of *and* when you write 'between [this year] and [this year]', because that mixture of a word and a symbol would spoil the parellel construction. You are probably familiar with the convention of relating academic and fiscal years in the form 2002–03, but when describing historical dates, it is more common in Religious Studies to give all of the digits for the concluding year. This prevents confusion when relating years before the Common Era. When authors consistently omit from the terminal year the digits that do not change, we cannot tell, for instance, whether 225–21 BCE refers to four years or 204 years:

Not Preferred: 1950–53; 1980–92; 1250–40 BCE
Preferred: 1950–1953; 1980–1992; 1250–1240 BCE
Wrong: between 1950–1953; from 1980–1992
Right: between 1950 and 1953; from 1980 to 1992

Scholarly Abbreviations

What follows are the most common Latin and English abbreviations used by scholars.

Latin Abbreviations

Abbreviation	Latin Word	English Meaning
c. *or* ca.	circa	about, approximately
cf.	confer	compare
e.g. (*not* ex. *or* eg.)	exempli gratia	for example
et al.	et alia	and others
etc.	et cetera	and so on
fl.	floruit	flourished
ibid.	ibidem	in the same place
i.e. (*not* ie.)	id est	that is
MS *and* MSS	manuscriptum	manuscript(s)
s.v.	sub voce	see under
viz.	videlicet	namely

The abbreviations **cf.**, **e.g.**, **etc.**, **i.e.** and **viz.** are properly confined to notes or to parentheses within the essay body, so use their English equivalents elsewhere. **Viz.** ('namely') is not commonly used, so I do not encourage you to use it, but you should know what it means. The four other abbreviations just mentioned are very common. **Cf.** introduces a point of comparison. It does not simply mean 'see also' but 'see, by way of comparison'. Use **e.g.** and **i.e.** *before* the items they describe, in contrast with **etc.**, which has to occur at the end of a list of items. When **etc.** occurs at the end of a sentence, the abbreviating period doubles as the period for the sentence. The same is true for other abbreviations that precede periods. If for some strange reason the terminal punctuation following an abbreviation is an exclamation mark or a question mark, use both the abbreviating period and the terminal punctuation. As a rule of thumb, a sentence never terminates with two periods.

Given that **e.g.** means 'for example' and **etc.** means 'and so on', it would be redundant to preface a list with **e.g.** and conclude it with **etc.**, for they both indicate that the list is not comprehensive. Choose one or the other. When the list is exhaustive, the appropriate introductory abbreviation is **i.e.** ('that is'). It would be illogical to use **e.g.** to introduce all possible examples; indeed, it would be deceptive if done to imply that the few examples that exist to support a claim could be multiplied.

The abbreviations **c.** (or **ca.**) and **fl.** (for 'circa' and 'flourished') are used in connection with dates. The former precedes an approximate year or ranges of years. The latter introduces the years during which a person or school flourished. It is generally used when the chronology is otherwise obscure. These abbreviations usually appear in parentheses, although **c.** sometimes appears in the essay body. Both **et cetera** and **circa** have been adopted into the English language, so you can use the full word in place of **etc.** and **c.**

The abbreviations **et al.** ('and others'), **ibid.** ('in the same place') and **s.v.** ('see under') are properly confined to footnotes and endnotes. Writers sometimes use **s.v.** followed by a word or title in quotation marks when referring their readers to an entry in a dictionary or an encyclopedia. This convention makes sense if the entries in the book are in alphabetical order and the pagination varies in different print formats or across editions. When citing a secondary source that has more than three authors or editors, writers usually shorten the citation by listing the first author followed by **et al.** (note that *et* has no period). To save space and limit redundancy when citing the same work twice in a row, writers sometimes use **ibid.** for the second entry. Because **ibid.** always refers to the immediately preceding item, it cannot be used when a different work is cited in between. Like any abbreviation, **ibid.** is capitalized if it begins the entry. When **ibid.** refers not only to the same work as the preceding item but also to the same page(s), it appears alone. If the page or pages are different, add a comma after **ibid.**, the page or page range, and a terminal period. Of course, if the next and subsequent citations are also to the same work, **ibid.** does not decrease redundancy. Most style manuals now recommend against the use of **ibid.**, encouraging the use of a shortened title in its place (the section 'Methods of Documentation' explains this convention). A shortened title spares the reader the nuisance of checking the preceding note to learn what source is being cited and prevents erroneous citations that result when a new note is inserted between a note using **ibid.** and the note it refers back to.

Although not an abbreviation, the word **idem** ('the same') also appears in notes, where it means 'the same person previously mentioned'. Thus it sometimes replaces the name of the author in a list of works by the same person. Another full Latin word that you might encounter is **passim**, which means 'throughout' or 'here and there'. Authors use **passim** to indicate that a subject occurs frequently throughout a work. This information is not very helpful unless the author lists some pages worth reading before adding 'and passim'.

English Abbreviations

Abbreviation	Meaning
b.	born
BCE *or* B.C.E. (small caps or large caps)	before the Common Era
CE *or* C.E. (small caps or large caps)	the Common Era
chap. *and* chaps.	chapter *and* chapters
col. *and* cols.	column *and* columns
d.	died
ed. *and* eds.	editor *and* editors; edition
esp.	especially
f. *and* ff.	and the following
n. *and* nn.	note *and* notes
n.d.	no date
no. *and* nos.	number *and* numbers
n.p.	no place; no publisher
n.s.	new series
p. *and* pp.	page *and* pages
trans.	translator
v. *and* vv.	verse *and* verses
vol. *and* vols	volume *and* volumes

The abbreviations BCE and CE (replacing BC and AD) follow dates and are necessary only when the context does not make it clear to which era you are referring. BCE and CE can be used anywhere in the essay, as can **b.** ('born') and **d.** ('died'), which, however, must appear in parentheses. Much like **c.** and **fl.**, **b.** and **d.** precede years. Most of the other English abbreviations listed above are confined to footnotes.

Notice that the correct abbreviations for *page* and *pages* are **p.** and **pp.** (*not* pg.). It is incorrect to write out the full word *page* as part of documentation, but you would use the full word rather than the abbreviation within a sentence, as in this example: 'The author discusses this subject here and in the pages that follow.' Some style manuals deem these abbreviations unnecessary except where the reader might be uncertain whether the number denotes a page.

When citing more than one page of secondary literature or a passage of scripture, scholars sometimes note the first page or verse then tack on **f.** or **ff.** The singular **f.** means 'and the one that follows', whereas **ff.** means 'and the ones that follow'. Scholars use the latter when they cannot decide where the passage logically ends or just cannot be bothered to check. So, for example, Katha Upanishad I.1.12f. is the same thing as Katha Upanishad I.1.12–13, whereas Katha Upanishad I.1.12ff. means: Start reading at Katha Upanishad I.1.12 and stop reading when the passage no longer seems relevant to my point. Since **ff.** is not very helpful to a reader and encourages imprecision and laziness among authors, these two abbreviations are no longer acceptable. If you encounter a scholar who uses **ff.** for pages, you have cause to wonder whether that person reread those pages before citing them, and accurately recalls their contents.

Conciseness

There is relatively little time to write essays in the first years of university, so many students are happy just to get them done on time. In later years, students often find themselves devoting more time to writing more substantial term papers and becoming increasingly critical of their efforts, finding their writing verbose, convoluted, and tedious. If you are in this situation and still have time to devote to your paper, you should edit it for conciseness, particularly if you have written more than the assigned maximum. Read each sentence and ask yourself: Can I say this in fewer words? If you did not hit upon the right verb when writing a sentence, you probably ended up using helper verbs and adverbs or a lengthy noun phrase. Consider this example:

> The three 'rafts' of Buddhism all revere a single founder from whom they claim their teachings derive.[7]

In this sentence, all of the words following the verb *revere* function as the direct object. Are they all necessary? It would be difficult in this case to find one noun that conveys the same thought, but the problem here is the verb *revere*, which is not the true focus of the sentence. Thus we could shorten the sentence by finding the correct verb and eliminating unnecessary adjectives:

> All three 'rafts' of Buddhism attribute their teachings to the same founder.

Sometimes the difference between the right verb and a cumbersome phrase can be dramatic. Consider the difference between 'the priest would not provide an explanation for his actions' and 'the priest would not explain his actions'. Although the wordiness of the former clause sounds typically academic, the real objective of academic language is clarity and precision, and clarity is always enhanced by using no more words than necessary. Although time consuming, this kind of editing can decrease the length of your essay by 10 per cent or more without sacrificing any substance.

A large amount of technical-sounding verbiage results from using the weak verb *to be* together with a phrase in place of one strong verb. This painful periphrasis is not hard to spot and eliminate. Here are some examples:

Wordy	Better
Taoists have a tendency to be lovers of nature.	Taoists tend to love nature. Taoists generally love nature.
Dharma is in accordance with karma.	Dharma accords with karma.
The focus of this essay is on a topic that is becoming a burning issue, namely, the ordination of gay priests.	This essay focuses on the burning issue of the ordination of gay priests.

The Torah is in danger of being rendered obsolete.	The Torah could become obsolete.
This is a painful realization that could lead to doubt.	This painful realization could lead to doubt.

You will probably find many places in your paper where you said basically the same thing in two consecutive sentences because you felt that your first sentence did not quite convey what you meant. In these cases, eliminate the unnecessary wordiness in both sentences, and then revise them into one sentence that expresses the thought that you inadequately conveyed in your first attempt.

Notes

[1] An exception occurs in running text when a quotation that breaks off with a period or comma in the source is followed in your essay by a parenthetical citation of the source. In such cases, the period or comma is moved to the right of the parenthetical citation in order to avoid a double period or comma.

[2] The original dedication that inspired this example was long thought to be untraceable, but thanks to Google Book Search I was able to locate its likely source in a matter of seconds: Robert Mills Bevensee, *Electromagnetic Slow Wave Systems* (New York: Wiley, 1964). Bevensee's dedication reads, 'This Book Is Dedicated to my parents, Ayn Rand, and the glory of GOD' (line breaks follow the word 'to' and each comma).

[3] All translations of the Gospel of Matthew are from the New English Translation (NET Bible), a heavily annotated utility that is currently free to use and to download at http://www.bible.org/netbible/.

[4] Ramanada Prasad, trans., *The Bhagavad Gita*, International Gita Society, http://www.gita4free.com/english_completegita.html.

[5] As translated in James Legge, *The Chinese Classics: With a Translation, Critical and Exegetical Notes, Prolegomena and Copious Indexes*, 2nd rev. edn (Oxford: Clarendon, 1893), vol. 1 (punctuation slightly modified).

[6] Chicago Editorial Staff, *The Chicago Manual of Style*, 15th edn (Chicago: University of Chicago Press, 2003), 460.

[7] Modified from Huston Smith, *The World's Religions* (San Francisco: HarperSanFrancisco, 1991), 144.

4 The Hallmarks of Bad Scholarship: Considerations for Advanced Students

No one becomes a scholar simply by reading other people's essays and forming opinions about them. In order to know a subject as a scholar, you need to do what scholars do: structure your haphazard thoughts logically and systematically in essays. Your professors' lectures and the scholarly essays you read will be your guides to how to think and argue like a scholar. Unfortunately, not all scholarship deserves to be emulated. Knowing the characteristics of bad scholarship will help you identify and disavow inept, disingenuous, or apologetic research.

One cause of bad scholarship is a scholar's commitment to problematic conclusions. This situation happens for a variety of reasons. Sometimes scholars discover intractable problems with their theories so far along in the process of composing their case that they cannot face starting over. So they refuse to confront the problems. Many find it hard to acknowledge errors in their publications, so they continue to defend their erroneous statements and disproved theories in an effort to save face. Many allow their religious or ideological beliefs to determine the boundaries of acceptable conclusions. When a theory that challenges these beliefs becomes popular, these scholars become apologists; they take it upon themselves to discredit that theory (and the people who hold it) regardless of how well it explains the evidence. Some play king of the hill, treating other scholars as rivals for their spot on the summit rather than as collaborators. Then there are the scholars who think they have made an exciting discovery that will revolutionize the way we see something. Enthralled by its implications, they grab hold of a bad idea and run with it. Even the best scholars sometimes develop a crazy pet theory and proclaim it fervently despite the universal disinterest or disapproval of their colleagues, like a voice crying out in the wilderness.

Intellectual laziness is another cause of bad scholarship. It takes a great deal of time and effort to produce studies that are impervious to criticism. The most important contributions are generally produced by scholars who have spent many years studying their subject and acquiring the background knowledge and technical skills to do so. Correspondingly, the worst contributions are generally produced by scholars who write on subjects they know little about. Reactionary scholarship tends to be of this sort. Scholars who have rigid ideas about what can and cannot be true see the obligation of responding to competing explanations as an inconvenience rather than as an opportunity to learn something new. They therefore put little effort into their refutations, often just repeating what other like-minded scholars have already said, accepting as fact whatever opinions they happen to like. You are not likely to produce an insightful and valuable reply to someone else's work without doing an equal amount of research on that subject.

Although the reasons for bad scholarship are highly individual, the results are fairly standard: scholars who are lazy or committed to problematic positions find ways to avoid arguments they cannot answer and evidence they cannot explain, and when they do confront the facts, they commit errors in reasoning (fallacies) through carelessness or the necessity of making their problematic positions appear plausible. Let us first look at how scholars avoid rationally engaging other scholars' arguments.

Pretend Refutations

Ad Hominem Attacks

Anyone who has watched political pundits 'debate' is familiar with the technique of discrediting the person instead of the arguments. Scholars do this too by finding ways to make their readers dislike or distrust the experts who disagree with them. Scholars sometimes portray each other as religious or ideological stereotypes (the angry feminist, the radical liberal, the unthinking fundamentalist), question each other's motives and intelligence, and expose each other's hypocrisy. When faced with rational criticism of their own ideas, they sometimes misrepresent the criticism (straw-man arguments) or enunciate the motives behind it rather than answer it. These rhetorical attempts to discredit the source of an argument are intellectually vacuous, for the validity of an argument is logically separate from the integrity of the person who makes it.

Exposés of the personal motives, biases, or cultural con-ditioning of a person who makes an argument deserve special attention because these dispositions might appear to be more relevant. This more civil means of shifting the issue from the argument to the person is no less fallacious, however, because the reason a person subscribes to a particular view is no more relevant to its truth than that person's character. We are all products of our societies, biased in our own peculiar ways, yet capable of devising defensible positions. Our peculiar biases help us perceive facts that others might not notice, even as they blind us to facts that seem obvious to most everyone else. Hence pointing out the biases of the people you disagree with does nothing to prove them wrong. However, once you have shown on intellectual grounds that a position is untenable, you might have cause to discuss the biases of the scholars who hold it, provided their acceptance seems so odd to your way of thinking that it cries out for explanation.

People are sometimes unsure about the legitimacy of ad

hominem arguments due to the fact that they are integral to legal prosecution, which, like scholarship, is supposed to be a means of discovering the truth. Matters of motive and bias become relevant in the courtroom because much of the evidence consists of unverifiable statements from expert and lay witnesses. Whenever a witness testifies to matters that the jurors cannot verify, it is quite legitimate for the lawyers to question the witness's credibility. Fortunately, in scholarship, unverifiable claims are rarely at issue.

Straw-man Opponents

One of the easiest and therefore most common ways to refute a scholar's position without engaging it is through caricature. Instead of accurately describing what a scholar argued, apologists often latch on to one aspect of the thesis that sounds silly or offensive and treat it as the essence of their opponent's thesis. Some of the silliest academic positions you will read about are not in fact the positions of the scholars being ridiculed but polemical distortions that have been so successful that few people now read the original work and know what the scholar really argued. Scholars also battle straw men when they refuse to acknowledge their strongest opponents and instead take on the weak ones, pretending thereby to have won a victory for their position.

Stereotyped Opponents

Through the magic of generalization, straw-man arguments are readily applied to groups of scholars. When several scholars defend the same basic position in different ways, it is tempting to paint them all with the same brush, ignoring their good arguments while characterizing all of them as believing the least plausible positions held among them. Here is an example:

> Proponents of [the secret Gospel of Mark], on the other hand, have contended that Carpocrates's teaching repre- sents an early version of Mark, prior to what is in the New

Testament, and that Jesus and his followers engaged in esoteric – and sexual – practices.[1]

This statement supposedly describes the positions of all scholars who believe that the 'secret' Gospel of Mark is an early Christian document, but in reality not all of these scholars believe that this text predates the Gospel of Mark that is found in the Bible, only one scholar supposed that the heretic Carpocrates had a hand in editing Mark's gospel (and even that scholar did not believe that any of Carpocrates's teaching remains in the Gospel of Mark), and only one (serious) scholar deemed it *possible* that Jesus engaged in sexual practices. The kernel of truth is what makes such misrepresentations sound plausible.

Misquotation

This form of intellectual dishonesty is common in straw-man arguments. Apologists and other scholars engaged in polemics sometimes misrepresent the positions of their opponents by quoting them out of context and occasionally by omitting words that would put the quotation in a proper light. Usually disdain leads scholars to misquote their opponents in this way. Occasionally, however, scholars inadvertently misquote someone when they honestly misunderstand that person's point and accordingly misrepresent the context of the quotation. They occasionally even change some of the words in the quotation, inadvertently recording words they expected to see and not the words that the person wrote. The simple remedy for this problem is to check your quotations against the original work at the proofreading stage.

Cavalier dismissal

Apart from ignoring arguments altogether, the easiest way of avoiding the responsibility of intellectual engagement is by dismissing arguments as ignorant, ridiculous, or fantastic. The famous historian Morton Smith, for instance, dismissed early literary-critical studies of the Gospel of Mark as 'principally interesting as examples of the extravagance of exegetic fantasy needed to transform "Mark" from an editor – or a series of editors – to an author'. Likewise, in the course of arguing that the story of Jesus' transfiguration was based on a real, but hypnotically induced, vision, Smith commented, 'A review of the other "explanations" proposed for the transfiguration story would be a waste of time; they are chiefly of interest as evidence of the proponents' ignorance.'[2] People who resort to derision channel their acumen into making their dismissals sound clever, but clever is not the same thing as true, and the mere assertion that a position is not worth rebutting proves nothing. As D. A. Carson pointed out, 'Often what is meant by such cavalier dismissal is that the opposing opinion emerges from a matrix of thought so different from a scholar's own that he finds it strange, weird, and unacceptable (unless he changes his entire framework).'[3]

Generally speaking, if scholars can refute other explanations, they do, so when they dismiss arguments without being able to explain what is wrong with them, they are cheating themselves of an opportunity to see through different eyes. Still, some explanations really are so weak that they do not merit rebuttal in an essay (Smith's explanation of the transfiguration is a good example). Ideally, one should critique any theory that is intelligent enough that it has – or likely will – become influential, and any unintelligent theory that is nevertheless taken seriously by scholars. A theory that is so quirky that no scholar except its creator accepts it can be passed over, either in silence or with the polite observation that it has not commanded assent.

Cavilling dismissal

Although spelled nearly the same as the preceding heading, a caviller or cavilling dismissal is accomplished through trivial or frivolous objections. It is another form of the straw-man argument, insofar as people who raise trivial objections to a thesis do not acknowledge any good supporting arguments that they cannot answer. That is, rather than describing their opponents' arguments then answering them systematically, they imply that their opponents' arguments consist entirely of whatever trivial problems they managed to expose. Such nit-picking usually occurs haphazardly in footnotes that mention only the specific points that the scholar can counter. That way the nit-picker can avoid acknowledging that the scholar in question actually has a thesis which these frivolous objections do not answer. People who engage in this pretend form of debate respond to criticism of their own positions the same way, by suppressing any important objections that they cannot answer.

Footnote dismissal

It is not possible, or desirable, to prove everything in an essay, so scholars will occasionally use a footnote to refer the reader to additional research that they believe settles a disputed issue in their favour. When scholars are honest, these footnotes cite research that sufficiently refutes a contrary position or answers all of the important objections to their preferred position. Too often, however, the scholarship cited in these footnotes consists of similar evasions of argument by scholars who share the same bias. The pretence that a list of like-minded scholars settles an issue amounts to phoney documentation, yet scholars do this kind of thing all the time. They have little to worry about, for very few people know a subject well enough to recognize when the totality of sources cited in a note does not constitute the alleged proof.

Fallacies of Argument

Now that we are more familiar with the standard tricks that scholars use to persuade without arguing, let us turn to the common mistakes they make when they do argue.

Treating what Is Possible as Proved

A chain of reasoning is only as strong as its weakest link. Hence, it is best to build an argument like a pyramid, with the most-secure premise or best-documented proposition as the foundation, upon which subsequent reasonable inferences can be based. Any inferences or premises that are merely possible should be left out of the chain of argument; if mentioned at all, they should not be presented as conclusions but as possibilities worth exploring. Frequently, however, scholars try to prove an unlikely point by constructing an argument on a premise that is merely possible. In order to do this, they quietly shift the way they describe the premise. At first they describe it as possible. Later on, they omit the qualifiers, such as 'might' and 'could', and treat the premise as if it were securely established. Sometimes the transition from possible to certain is separated by intervening discussions, which give the reader time to forget how inadequately the premise was established. Refuting an argument built on a weak or demonstrably false premise is like cutting down a tree. You can ignore everything above the lower trunk. Just chop through the false premise and get safely out of the way.

Special Pleading

Scholars who are upfront about the fact that some aspect of their argument is improbable or unsubstantiated sometimes ask that an exception to the rules of evidence be made in this case, hoping that their readers will grant this problematic point because the rest of the case is good. These scholars may be commended for not committing the next three fallacies.

Selective Evidence

What is the best way to make a bad argument look good? Cite the evidence that supports it and omit the evidence that contradicts it or actually proves it false. Arguments that hide inconvenient information can easily impress readers who know little about the subject, but are readily demolished by anyone who looks behind the scholar's back. Of course, anyone who is accused of concealing facts can plead ignorance – selective ignorance of inconvenient facts. Naturally, most scholars do not want to be in the position of having others decide whether they are ignorant or dishonest. I would like to say that intellectual integrity is the principal reason competent scholars actively seek out disconfirming evidence in order to test their own theories, but fear of being embarrassed by more knowledgeable scholars is as strong a motivator.

Buried Concession

Instead of omitting inconvenient facts, scholars sometimes bury them in notes. This is easier to do in a book with hundreds of endnotes than in an article in which the notes are at the bottom of the page. Buried concessions are the academic equivalent of fine-print disclaimers – and just as disconcerting when discovered.

Erroneous or Phoney Documentation

As I noted under 'footnote dismissal', scholars sometimes substantiate claims with reference to scholarship that, when inspected, turns out not to contain the alleged demonstration. Frequently this error results from carelessness: a scholar mistakenly recollects that a particular study contains the requisite proof, confusing that study with ideas that occurred to him or her while reading it. Other times it results from conscientiousness. As scholars refine their arguments by rewriting paragraphs, they sometimes change the point made in a sentence, rendering the accompanying documentation invalid. The longer people work on a paper, the more mistakes creep into the documentation in this way. Those who take the time to check their documentation before publication by rereading the pages of the studies they cite know how often these mistakes happen. Occasionally, however, erroneous documentation is deliberate. Just as scientists sometimes tweak their data, scholars sometimes exaggerate or slant what another scholar has proved. So if an important assertion strikes you as dubious, look up the scholar's documentation.

A subtler and safer form of phoney documentation is facilitated by the imprecise connection between unelaborated bibliographical information and the sentence to which it is attached. The fact that the standard note format 'See Author's Name, *A Study That Sounds Relevant*, several pages' could apply to any element in the text that precedes it allows scholars to appear to substantiate an important assertion with reference to secondary literature that actually concerns something else. The secondary literature cited in the note might, for instance, substantiate an incidental point made in the same sentence or slightly earlier in the text, or merely comment on the point requiring documentation but prove nothing about it. Readers naturally *assume* that the note substantiates whatever claim is most important and in need of substantiation, but since this is an inference, they cannot cry foul when it turns out that the cited work concerns something else. When authors realize that their notes could mislead in this way, they should preface their documentation with a phrase stating what it concerns.

Discounting Contrary Evidence

All scholars do this. Faced with an inconvenient fact that their conscience cannot deny, they find reasons to discount it, assuming that if their thesis is correct, the problem must be more apparent than actual. There is nothing wrong with subjecting problematic facts to intense scrutiny to determine if they really are facts, but if, in the end, your reasons for discounting them are feeble, you are engaging in a form of special pleading. A better approach is either to acknowledge the fact and let the reader decide how great a problem it is or to modify the thesis in order to account for the fact. Scientific method requires the latter.

Excluding Unorthodox Evidence

The tendency of religiously committed scholars to exclude large bodies of evidence from their research is a major problem in Religious Studies. Many scholars subscribe to a 'golden age' theory of the origin of their own religion, supposing that the earliest period was characterized by doctrinal unanimity, which eventually deteriorated through the emergence of heretical groups that corrupted 'the One True Faith'. These scholars construe unorthodox texts and artifacts as aberrations and refuse to entertain the possibility that they originated in the earliest period and contain any reliable information about the origins of their religion. Thus, for example, although the early Christians produced at least thirty-two gospels, conservative Christian scholars treat only the four gospels in the New Testament as containing reliable information about Jesus and first-century Christianity. By excluding unorthodox evidence from their research, they ensure that their historical conclusions affirm the primacy (hence truth) of the doctrines that were eventually deemed orthodox. The inverse tendency occurs among liberal scholars, whose nonconformist religious beliefs incline them to give credence to texts that display theological diversity. These two biases, apocryphobia (unnatural aversion to non-canonical texts) and apocryphilia (unnatural attraction to non-canonical texts), are methodologically indefensible. One cannot determine a text's historical value without first studying it without prejudice. What scholars need to do is subject all the evidence – orthodox and unorthodox – to the same degree of scrutiny.

False Dilemma (False Dichotomy)

When comedian talk-show host Stephen Colbert used to provoke his guests with the question, 'George W. Bush – good president, or *great* president?' he was creating a false dilemma, forcing them to choose between two alternatives when others are possible. Scholars sometimes do this too, though less overtly. Arguing is much simpler if you can convince your readers that they must choose between your position and a position that you can prove false. Arguments based on a false dilemma are rendered dubious if even one other viable alternative exists.

Appeal to the Opinion of an Authority

One cannot substantiate a claim merely by quoting a scholar who makes it. If the claim is essential to your argument or a matter of dispute, you need to give your readers compelling reasons to accept it. The inadequacy of citing an opinion when reasons are required is not overcome by describing the scholar who holds that opinion as great or famous. If a matter has theological or ideological implications, weighty opinions about it come in all sizes and colours to suit any occasion. The fallaciousness of appeals to authority increases when authors single out the one or two authorities who share their opinion, as if the ones who disagree are irrelevant. Even more intellectually offensive are the authors who, instead of citing the published *reasons* of a 'great authority', cite only the *opinion* because those reasons have already been rebutted or are notably uncompelling.

I do not mean to imply that unargued opinions are never relevant to an essay. It is appropriate, for instance, to cite an authority's unargued opinion as part of the rationale for examining the merits of that opinion. Nor am I implying that opinions are like 'belly buttons' (everybody has one). Although they cannot substitute for reasons and evidence in an argument, the opinions of people who have spent years studying the subject at issue should never be lightly dismissed; they are the ones most worth investigating.

Appeal to Common sense and Self-evidence

Although people appeal to common sense nearly as often as they quote Noam Chomsky, common sense is not a recognized authority on anything. The truth about a matter may in fact be counterintuitive, confuting common sense. Hence be wary of claims touted as commonsensical or self-evident.

People tend to appeal to common sense or claim that something is self-evident precisely when they cannot find proof, so such phrases as 'everyone knows that', 'common sense dictates', and 'it is self-evident that' should sound warning bells when you read them. Note that I am not criticizing words such as 'clearly' and 'obviously' used as sentence adverbs to introduce sound logical inferences. I am objecting to the substitution of common sense and self-evidence for proof.

Appeal to Personal Experience and Subjective Knowledge

Personal anecdotes might be sufficient to prove that something occasionally happens, and can make for interesting illustrations of points that have been substantiated on other grounds, but personal experiences cannot substitute for evidence in an argument, because they are not open to inspection. Thus, for example, few people would object to my remarking 'My students frequently make this mistake' if that remark is not intended to prove something important. If, on the other hand, I began a paper with the assertion, 'We know that demonic possession is real because I have witnessed cases that defy psychological explanation', I would be basing my paper on a claim that I cannot prove.

Confusing Correlation with Causality

When two things regularly happen together, it is easy to suppose that one of them causes the other, but a causal relationship is not established by mere correlation. The two things that occur together might both be caused by something else. For example, if we were to grant the disputed assertion that people who go on murderous rampages also play violent video games, it would not follow that violent video games must be a contributing factor, because an interest in violent video games might only be a symptom of other problems that dispose a person to real-life violence. If violent video games were a cause of real-life violence, it would be difficult to explain why many people who play violent video games do not become more violent or even desensitized to violence in real life. If there is a relationship between violent video games and real-life violence, it must be more complicated than cause and effect.

Assuming the Conclusion (Begging the Question)
In this fallacy, an argument assumes as true that which it is offered to prove. Here is a typical example:

> Thesis: The Gospel of Matthew is based on the Gospel of Mark.
> Argument 1: Matthew follows Mark's sequence.
> Argument 2: Matthew uses 50 per cent of Mark's words but improves on Mark's rough style.
> Conclusion: Matthew used Mark as a source.

The two arguments that support this conclusion are both framed in a way that presumes the conclusion that Matthew used Mark. One can demonstrate that Matthew and Mark relate the same incidents using essentially the same sentences and agree for the most part in their sequence of materials, but these facts do not prove that Matthew used Mark. It remains possible that Mark used Matthew or that both authors used a third writing. Likewise, the fact that Matthew and Mark frequently use the same basic sentences when describing the same incidents but Matthew's writing is more polished than Mark's does not prove that Matthew used Mark. Again, both authors could have used a third source, or Mark could have revised Matthew's wording to accord with Mark's more colloquial style. It would be less fallacious to argue that an author would be more likely to improve another author's style than to make it coarser. But that argument would constitute an appeal to common sense unless accompanied by evidence of the actual practices of ancient Greek authors.

Argument from Silence

Here the lack of evidence against a conclusion is offered as support for that conclusion. For example, some people argue that because Jesus denounced many sins but not homosexuality, he did not consider homosexuality to be a sin. Stated this way, the argument is fallacious, because there could be many reasons for Jesus' silence about homosexuality, such as the likelihood that it was uncommon among Jews in his society. Moreover, the surviving gospels do not contain everything Jesus said. It is possible that he did express an opinion on this subject but his opinion either was never committed to writing or was recorded in a writing that is now lost. Would it be legitimate to infer from the gospels' silence that Jesus (and everyone else in the gospels) never had a bowel movement? The question we need to ask is: should we expect that kind of information in our available sources? On the issue of homosexuality, the fact that no surviving gospel records Jesus' opinion does constitute *weak* evidence in support of the position that he did not consider homosexuality to be a sin, since some other Jews of his day did denounce (Greek) homosexuality. One would need to consider that weak evidence alongside the stronger evidence that Jesus presumed that marriage occurs between a man and a woman and considered sex outside of marriage to be a sin (Mt. 5:27–28, 31–32; 19:3–12). In general, arguments from silence are not worth making unless the silence of our sources is very surprising.

Evaluative Double Standards

In an ideal world, scholars would always compare competing theories against each other and provisionally accept the one that best accounts for the relevant facts, regardless of its implications. In the real world, scholars tend to accept the theory that comports best with their broad picture of the field, allowing their gut feelings and accumulated wisdom to influence their assessments, like a butcher who weighs a cut of beef with his fingers resting on the scale. When they weigh the evidence before their readers, they subconsciously tamper with the scales, often by making the burden of proof very low for the preferred theory (they list only the strengths) and impossibly high for all the others (they list only the weaknesses, treating any problem, however trivial, as fatal). By applying an evaluative double standard, the disfavoured theories are disqualified for not being perfect, and the favoured theory, not having been subjected to rigorous examination, wins by default.

Avoiding Bad Scholarship

Many of the dodges I have described are hard to detect. How, for instance, do you know whether the documentation in footnote 18 is legitimate unless you look it up? At this point in your studies you do not have the time or opportunity to verify everything yourself, but you should check the documentation that scholars offered for claims that are important to your own essay. When you must place your complete trust in scholars, choose the ones who are most qualified *on that subject* over more famous ones in the same field. People who have studied a subject for a dozen years usually know what they are talking about. Be extremely sceptical about *any* characterization of the issues that appears in a reply from a morally offended apologist. When you notice rhetoric, forms of evasion, and other tell-tale signs of bad scholarship in a particular work, you would be wise not to trust the author.

Most of the forms of bad scholarship that I outlined result from intellectual laziness and a commitment to inadequate explanations. It follows that the surest way to avoid these intellectual pitfalls in your own research is by being extremely thorough and open-minded, making discovery of the truth, not the protection of received or preconceived truth, your principal goal. For our purposes, the truth is not something metaphysical that is 'out there' but simply the best current explanation of a phenomenon, the one that can account for all of the facts that are presently available and recognized to be relevant by people who share the same set of presuppositions. This sort of truth is not One but multifaceted, so a variety of methodologies and presuppositions can lead to conclusions that are different but still complementary and true. That is not to say that any thesis is in some sense true and valid. There are strong theses that leave nothing unaccounted for, demonstrably false theses, and everything in between. You may never discover the truth about a particular issue, but you can keep moving towards it by actively seeking out and confronting facts that your thesis cannot explain, and by modifying or thoroughly revising your thesis until it is completely adequate.

If you have a strong conscience, you know when your thesis is not quite adequate. A little voice in your head objects when you avoid confronting an issue or fact or commit an intellectual fallacy. You hope that years from now that little voice will become proudly silent. The secret is to pay attention to that voice and not stifle it. It might help, now and then, to print up your paper and read through it with scepticism, putting an asterisk in the margin every time you hear that voice. Then turn to those asterisks, make a list of the problems, and devote your attention to them.

A Few Final Thoughts

If there is one conviction that pervades this guide, it is this: essay writing is not just a way of expressing your views. It is a process that structures your thinking, allowing you to turn random insights and interesting ideas into cogent, testable theories. If practised with an open mind and intellectual integrity, it is a remedy against the human penchant to believe what we want to believe, a way forward towards – we hope – the truth. Writing essays is one of the best ways to master a subject, and mastering essay writing is an integral part of becoming a scholar. Give it a fair try: the greater insight you acquire will more than reward your effort.

Notes

[1] Bruce Chilton, 'Unmasking a False Gospel', *The New York Sun*, October 25, 2006.

[2] Morton Smith, *Clement of Alexandria and a Secret Gospel of Mark* (Cambridge, MA: Harvard University Press, 1973), 97; idem, 'The Origin and History of the Transfiguration Story', *Union Seminary Quarterly* 31 (1980): 41.

[3] D. A. Carson, *Exegetical Fallacies* (Grand Rapids: Baker Book House, 1984), 120. I borrowed this topic and its title from Carson's discussion.

Select Bibliography

Style Guides

Alexander, Patrick H., et al. *The SBL Handbook of Style: For Ancient Near Eastern, Biblical, and Early Christian Studies*. Peabody, MA: Hendrickson, 1999.

The Chicago Manual of Style, 15th edn. Chicago: University of Chicago Press, 2003.

Greer, Michael. *What Every Student Should Know about Citing Sources with MLA Documentation*. New York: Pearson Longman, 2007.

MLA Handbook for Writers of Research Papers. Edited by Joseph Gibaldi. New York: Modern Language Association of America, 2003.

MLA Style Manual and Guide to Scholarly Publishing. 2nd edn. Edited by Joseph Gibaldi. New York: Modern Language Association of America, 1998.

Strunk, William, Jr, and E. B. White. *The Elements of Style*. Illustrated by Maira Kalman. New York: Penguin, 2005.

Trimmer, Joseph F. *A Guide to MLA Documentation: With an Appendix on APA Style*. 7th edn. Boston: Houghton Mifflin, 2006.

Turabian, Kate L. *A Manual for Writers of Research Papers, Theses, and Dissertations: Chicago Style for Students and Researchers*. 7th edn. Chicago: The University of Chicago Press, 2007.

Bibliographies and Indexes of Secondary Literature on Religion

General

ATLA Religion Database. Evanston, IL: American Theological Library Association, 1995–1998. Continued online through EBSCO Information Services.

Holm, Jean. *Keyguide to Information Sources on World Religions*. London and New York: Mansell, 1991.

Johnston, William M. *Recent Reference Books in Religion: A Guide for Students, Scholars, Researchers, Buyers, and Readers*. Rev. edn. Chicago: Fitzroy Dearborn, 1998.

Religious and Theological Abstracts. Myerstown, PA: Theological Publications, 1958–2004. Continued online.

Wilson, John Frederick, and Thomas P. Slavens. *Research Guide to Religious Studies*. Sources of Information in the Humanities 1. Chicago: American Library Association, 1982.

Christianity and Judaism

Catholic Periodical and Literature Index. Haverford, PA: Catholic Library Association, 1968–. Also available online through EBSCO Information Services.

Elenchus of Biblica. Roma: Editrice Pontificio Istituto biblico, 1968–.

Glynn, John. *Commentary & Reference Survey: A Comprehensive Guide to Biblical and Theological Resources*. Grand Rapids: Kregel Academic & Professional, 2007.

Index theologicus (IxTheo). Zeitschrifteninhaltsdienst Theologie der Universitätsbibliothek Tübingen. Also available online.

Index to Jewish Periodicals. Beachwood, OH. 1963–. Also available online through EBSCO Information Services.

Jewish Abstracts. New York: MBRS Information Services, 1996–1999.

Kepple, Robert J., and John R. Muether. *Reference Works for Theological Research*. 3rd edn. Lanham: University Press of America, 1991.

Mills, Watson E. *Bibliographies for Biblical Research: Periodical Literature for the Study of the New Testament*. Lewiston, NY: Mellen Biblical Press, 2002–.

———. *Bibliographies for Biblical Research: Periodical Literature for the Study of the Old Testament*. Lewiston, NY: Mellen Biblical Press, 2002–.

Minor, Mark. *Literary-Critical Approaches to the Bible: An Annotated Bibliography*. West Cornwall, CT: Locust Hill, 1992.

———. *Literary-Critical Approaches to the Bible: A Bibliographical Supplement*. West Cornwall, CT: Locust Hill, 1996.

New Testament Abstracts. Weston, MA: Weston College of the Holy Spirit, 1956–. Also available online through EBSCO Information Services.

Old Testament Abstracts. Washington, DC: Catholic Biblical Association of America, 1978–. Also available online through EBSCO Information Services.

Powell, Mark Allan. *The Bible and Modern Literary Criticism: A Critical Assessment and Annotated Bibliography.* New York: Greenwood, 1992.

RAMBI: The Index of Articles on Jewish Studies, http://jnul.huji.ac.il/rambi/.

Wagner, Günter. *An Exegetical Bibliography of the New Testament.* Macon, GA: Mercer University Press, 1983–.

East Asian Religions

Bibliography of Asian Studies. Ann Arbor: Association for Asian Studies, 1941–1991. Continued online: http://www.aasianst.org/bassub.htm.

Earhart, H. B. *The New Religions of Japan: A Bibliography of Western-Language Materials.* 2nd edn. Ann Arbor: Center for Japanese Studies, University of Michigan, 1983.

Farmer, Edward L., Romeyn Taylor, and Ann Waltner. *Ming History: An Introductory Guide to Research.* Ming Studies Research Series 3. Minneapolis: University of Minneapolis History Department, 1995.

Fu, Charles Wei-hsun, and Wing-tsit Chan. *Guide to Chinese Philosophy.* Boston: G. K. Hall, 1978.

Loewe, Michael. *Early Chinese Texts: A Bibliographical Guide.* Early China Special Monograph Series 2. Berkeley: Society for the Study of Early China: Institute of East Asian Studies, University of California, Berkeley, 1993.

Pas, Julian F. *A Select Bibliography on Taoism.* IASWR Bibliographical Monographs 1. Stony Brook, NY: Institute for Advanced Studies of World Religions, 1988.

Schwade, Arcadio. *Shinto-Bibliography in Western Languages: Bibliography on Shinto and Religious Sects, Intellectual Schools and Movements Influenced by Shintoism.* Leiden: Brill, 1986.

Seaman, Gary, ed. *Chinese Religions: Publications in Western Languages.* 4 vols. Compiled by Gary Seaman, Laurence G. Thompson, and Zhifang Song. Ann Arbor: Association for Asian Studies, 1993–2002.

Yu, David C. *Guide to Chinese Religion.* With contributions by Laurence G. Thompson. Boston: G. K. Hall, 1985.

——. *Religion in Postwar China: A Critical Analysis and Annotated Bibliography*. Westport, CT: Greenwood, 1994.

Islam

Geddes, Charles L. *Guide to Reference Books for Islamic Studies*. Bibliographic Series, American Institute of Islamic Studies 9. Denver: American Institute of Islamic Studies, 1985.

Index Islamicus. East Grinstead, England: Bowker-Saur, 1994–. Also available online through Cambridge Scientific Abstracts and EBSCO Information Services.

Israeli, Raphael, with Lyn Gorman. *Islam in China: A Critical Bibliography*. Westport, CT: Greenwood, 1994.

Skreslet, Paula Youngman. *The Literature of Islam: A Guide to the Primary Sources in English Translation*. Lanham, MD: Scarecrow, 2006.

Buddhism, Hinduism, Jainism and Sikhism

Bibliography of Asian Studies. Ann Arbor: Association for Asian Studies, 1941–1991. Continued online: http://www.aasianst.org/bassub.htm.

Dell, David J., et al. *Guide to Hindu Religion*. Boston: G. K. Hall, 1981.

Fenton, John Y. *South Asian Religions in the Americas: An Annotated Bibliography of Immigrant Religious Traditions*. Westport, CT: Greenwood, 1995.

Gulati, S. P., Rajinder Singh, Jasmer Singh, and Dalbir Singh, eds. *Bibliography of Sikh Studies*. 2 vols. Delhi: National Book Shop, 1989.

Inada, Kenneth K., ed. *Guide to Buddhist Philosophy*. With contributions by Richard Chi, Shotaro Iida, and David Kalupahana. Boston: G. K. Hall, 1985.

Potter, Karl H., ed. *Encyclopedia of Indian Philosophies*. 3rd rev. ed. 12 vols to date. Delhi: Motilal Banarsidass, 1995. An updated version of the first volume of bibliography exists online: http://faculty.washington.edu/kpotter/.

Potter, Karl H., with Austin B. Creel and Edwin Gerow. *Guide to Indian Philosophy*. Asian Philosophies and Religions Resource Guides. Boston: G. K. Hall, 1988.

Rai, Priya Muhar. *Sikhism and the Sikhs: An Annotated Bibliography*. Bibliographies and Indexes in Religious Studies 13. New York: Greenwood, 1989.

Reynolds, Frank E., John Holt, and John Strong, eds. *Guide to Buddhist Religion*. Arts selection by Bardwell Smith with Holly Waldo and Jonathan Clyde Glass. Boston: G. K. Hall, 1981.

Satyaprakash, ed. *Buddhism: A Select Bibliography*. Subject Bibliography Series 1. 2nd enlarged and revised edition. Gurgaon, Haryana: Indian Documentation Service, 1986.

———. *Hinduism: A Select Bibliography*. Subject Bibliography Series 4. Compiled by Syed Mohammed Ali and H. S. Sharma. Gurgaon, Haryana: Indian Documentation Service, 1984.

———. *Jainism: A Select Bibliography*. Subject Bibliography Series 6. Gurgaon, Haryana: Indian Documentation Service, 1984.

Singh, Rajwant, with Navneet Lamba. *The Sikhs: Their Literature, Culture, History, Philosophy, Politics, Religion, and Traditions*. Delhi: Indian Bibliographies Bureau, 1989.

Stietencron, Heinrich von, et al., eds. *Epic and Purāṇic Bibliography (to 1985): Annotated and with Indexes*. Purāṇa Research Publications, Tübingen. 3 vols. Wiesbaden: Otto Harrassowitz, 1992.

Index